# Incapable of
# Letting Go

**Jo Whitney Outland**

PAGE PUBLISHING, INC.
Conneaut Lake, PA

First originally published by Page Publishing 2020

ISBN 978-1-6624-1430-5 (pbk)
ISBN 978-1-6624-1431-2 (digital)

Printed in the United States of America

Rosemary's Senior year in high school

For my wonderful mother, Rosemary Wilkinson Outland, and to all those individuals who loved and so diligently stood by me during this entire situation.

"The moment we get tired in the waiting, God's spirit is right along-side helping us along. If we don't know how or what to pray, it doesn't matter. He does our praying in and for us, making prayer out of our worthless sighs, our aching groans. He knows us far better than we know ourselves."

—Romans 8:26–27

# ABOUT THE TITLE

I chose the title, *Incapable of Letting Go*, for several reasons. All these words describe the central situation in which I found myself when unable to accept my precious mother's death. According to *Webster's Basic English Dictionary*, the word *capable* signifies "having the ability or capacity to do something." Therefore, I was not capable of handling the death of the person closest to me on earth. The whole scenario of this event is depicted in this book, and the various reasons for my unacceptance are included. The entire situation was bizarre, unexpected, scary, and noteworthy—among many other words of description. It is, however, a story of truth whose details do more than simply explain a happening. In fact, they fully describe, in addition to other things, the role that the media and the legal system can both play during such an incidence. It is also a written account of how many individuals react to death in uncertain and unusual manners. Every person is different, and each reaction is too. I know because I experienced the event firsthand, and despite all the beauty and ugliness surrounding it, I have survived in ways and circumstances that are unbelievable and amazing to me.

"You make known to me the path of life."
                              —Proverbs 16:11

# CONTENTS

# My Reason for Writing This Book

I wrote this book to demonstrate how individuals accept or handle death when they react to the event itself. I also wish to reveal the many lessons that can be derived from experiencing such a situation as this one.

Also, the purpose of these writings is simply to detail a bizarre but very real story in my own life. One of its purposes too is to explain what can happen when an individual loses one of the closest persons in the world with whom she has a true relationship. In fact, the book describes an everyday occurrence of life ending, while it also details the uncertain and fearful situations that can go hand in hand with that happening—unusual and terrific as they may be.

I wrote about my experience because I wished to show that things are not what they often seem to be on the surface. There can always be more pertinent information surrounding an event that explains details even more. In the book too the importance of privacy is also mentioned and explained later. I, furthermore, chose to write about these topics because they detail the incidences, explained by me—a human being, who has taken steps to overcome a tragic thing and to gain strength from a divine being, God himself—to survive my own crises in life, following the initial tragedy that developed. Therefore, this book, *Incapable of Letting Go*, is a testimony—my personal and spiritual testimony—of making it through the worst times that life has to offer.

# CHAPTER ONE

# The Early Beginnings

Train up a child in the way he should go; even
when he is old he will not depart from it.
—Proverbs 22:6

When I was a child, Saturday was my favorite day of the week for one special reason. It was the time that Mom and I had an all-day outing with a trip downtown. Our city was small, and it had several stores, side by side, in rows. These were various kinds of shops, ranging from furniture stores to dime stores. This too was one of the days in the week Mom had an off day from her job or jobs that she had to support us. I looked forward to this downtown adventure because it often began with a city bus ride or a cab ride to downtown. I found these modes of transportation exciting and looked forward to being the one on the bus who pulled the "string" to let the bell ring, letting the driver know where to let us off on the ride. I guess, as a child, I felt proud to execute this duty, and especially to see all passengers, usually a motley crew, turn around to see who was planning to descend first and where.

Once downtown, I looked forward to picking the restaurant from which we would share our lunch. Mom used to say, "Joni Walker, what will it be today?" She called me by my first and middle name because that was what she always wanted everyone else to do. It never happened that way though because "Joni" was short enough and easy enough for everyone to say. I too knew that restaurant answer in advance, and I could almost taste the specialty of the day, whether it be hot dogs with chili and fries or turkey and dressing smothered with gravy on a piping-hot plate.

Sometimes too it was a julienne salad, laced with ham and cheese, and my favorite dressing—coincidentally Mom's too—Thousand Island. After lunch, we shopped for pleasure as well as necessity. I am sure that I liked the pleasure part best because I loved to see toys and other items that quickly captured my eyes as soon as we entered a store. If clothing was needed, however, I enjoyed that part too, since I could go to the dressing room and parade around in front of the mirror in order to pick what we liked best. A trip to the bookstore was one of my favorite places to go because, here, I could choose those pleasurable reading materials, and I really loved to read. My mom encouraged reading at an early age, and I believe it gave me knowledge that helped in latter school years.

I know too that reading, as to most people, gave me the escape from the real world momentarily, into a land of fantasy and the uncertain things to be. Mom allowed me to buy all the Nancy Drew mysteries, not all at once though. I know these books gave me joy, increased my fear, but always let me go to that world of sleuthing with all its eerie as well as made-up adventures. I learned also that these books as well as those involving Trixie Beldon, Kim Aldrich, and the Bobbsey Twins encouraged me to consider being a PI—private investigator—who solved whatever mysteries came my way. I even made a set of footprints out of white poster board, cut them out, and followed them to the best path that would lead me to what I needed to know. I also pulled out my trusty magnifying glass, which aided me in my search.

As a child, I found this to be an occupation or dream job of a lifetime and could not wait to solve the mystery at hand and be rewarded for doing so. The Cherry Ames book series, regarding a nurse, also made me consider being one, but a little later on, I knew that was not for me. *Too much blood and gory things*, I thought, even if the goal was to help people. Meanwhile, downtown with Mom, I even enjoyed going into one furniture store because upon entering, I got a free Coke, and that helped me to forget any boredom that I might endure, looking at all the household items that some adults seem to enjoy more than children. I took pleasure in going to the dime store the most, however, because I would often sway Mom to buy me at least one or two of those little knickknacks, such as jack rocks or Play-Doh, that kids love but do not necessarily need.

The last stop of the excursion was to purchase my "big prize" of the day to take home. It often included one of the following: a helium balloon, which eventually ended up in the sky before nighttime came; a punch ball, which was really noisy as I batted it back and forth, but usually lost air and went down to nothing by the end of the week; or a huge tissue-paper flower on a giant stick, which usually lasted longer than any, and which I cherished because I had already learned how to make a smaller version in the Girl Scouts. I loved to squirt real perfume on the tissue-paper pieces in order to give the flower a fragrance of its own. Nevertheless, these were prized possessions, all of them, and each one put the biggest smile upon my little-girl face, and it lasted for days at a time.

Every summer, when we were out of school, I remember vacation trips to Florida, accompanied by my mom, my maternal grandparents, my aunt, and my two first cousins. I loved these times too because I could see and play in the ocean, stay in a motel, and shop at some of the most unusual places along the waterfront. "A trip to the beach," I would always say when the days drew closer and closer to our destination. Although the car ride could be excessively long and brutally hot, I looked forward to the usual stops, on the way to and back, at different restaurants as well as at unique little stores whose decorations outside were as unique as those indoors. Sometimes, I saw all sorts of painted T-shirts and whatnots, and often too the beach toys—sand ones as well as blown-up animals, which were all over the place. Mom would always let me go to a local grocery store too, and it was fun to pick out any snacks or favorite drinks to keep on hand in a brand-new motel room where I could also watch television with the comfort of air-conditioning!

I remember two exceptional experiences that took place during two separate beach trips. Initially, the hotel that we occupied yearly always had special activities for the guests staying there. Once it was announced that a "penny dive" would be held for all the children in the motel pool itself. My mom and my aunt agreed to let my cousins and me participate. The object of the game was to dive in and collect as many coins as possible during a certain length of time. The funny thing occurred, however, when my mom instituted her water-safety rules that were always a component of beach trips or even activities at our local swimming pool. The motel required females to wear bathing caps, but my mom carried the safety rules a little even further by having me wear a life preserver for the event, the same one that I wore during trips to the ocean. I never thought about it at the time—what a hindrance this would be—but I do remember the disapproving look of the motel lifeguard in charge of the event itself.

What I mean is that my mom's safety requirement—the life preserver—wouldn't even enable me to gather any pennies for the contest because with it, it was impossible for me to dive, let alone look for pennies during the competition! Needless to say, I received no coins, while my female cousin got three or four. I was crushed, but common sense should have told me that Mom's safety rule ruined my chances of winning that day. Yet I did what she told me to because, in my eyes, Mom always told me the right thing to do, and I complied. She was correct too. I didn't drown.

The possibility of drowning did, however, come into the picture during another vacation at the beach. This experience was no laughing matter either. It was a sunny day, and I found myself sitting poolside at the deep end, sticking only my bare feet in the water. I had met some new female friends, and clothed in shorts and tops, we were innocently kicking a beach ball back and forth to one another in the water. In one split second I, probably distracted by the laughter and conversation of the time, actually forgot the kicking action and reached my hand in the pool to retrieve the beach ball. Unfortunately, I reached too far and fell into the deep end of the water. I'm sure I panicked for a moment or two, but I can remember that as I went under, I could see a male swimmer moving like a fish under the pool's diving board. That's mostly what I recall under the surface, but the truth was that at that time, I did not know how to swim. Unknown to me then too, I somehow pulled myself up to the top of the surface and held on tightly to the edge of the pool.

By then, and fortunately, one of my new friends had gone to get my mother, and just as I got myself up to the top of the water, she reached in and pulled me out in the rescue of a lifetime. Still in a state of shock and surprise, I held on to her with dear life and felt a strong sense of relief that is really unexplainable. Her face, full of extreme fear itself, changed to an expression of relief, but also of unbelief, at what had just occurred. I do remember never wanting to experience an event like that again. I also knew another thing—my mom saved me, but she mostly told everyone that I had the strength somehow to bring myself to the surface after going under the water. I am truly grateful for what we both were able to do that day, and I will never forget it as long as I live.

Holidays with my mom were quite special too. On Easter, we dressed in our Sunday's best, and after church, we had a huge egg hunt in the front yard of my grandparents' home. Besides collecting numerous eggs, the true prize of the day was to capture the golden egg, full of some unique treasure of its own and coveted by the finder more than anything else. We, of course, dyed real Easter eggs the night before. I especially loved writing my name on them with that special tool that somehow allowed my own name to appear after I dyed the eggs my favorite colors. Another big highlight of the morning was viewing what the Easter Bunny chose to bring us "good little girls and boys" as he hopped secretly into our house while we were sleeping. One of the most unusual and fun experiences was the Easter during which the hot temperatures got the best of the Bunny and the cherished basket gifts. Usually, the Bunny would fill up our baskets and place them across the living room floor. For some reason on this day, no signs of chocolate—chocolate eggs, chocolate bunnies, or chocolate crosses—could be found. My cousins and I were quite shocked, but then on the center living room table, we noticed a long piece of paper with a message scribbled on it. It was from the Easter Bunny himself!

Apparently, he explained, "During the long trip to the house, the chocolate bunnies melted because of the beaming sun in the sky." Therefore, he placed them in the refrigerator where they could get "good and cold" and be ready to eat shortly. We were elated. I think all of us children felt more special that time because we received a handwritten note—not just a note—but a note from the big Bunny himself, who took time to explain the unpleasant happening and how he worked to make it right for each one of us. We smiled, but I was personally satisfied because chocolate is my favorite, and I could not wait to get ahold of a piece!

When every single birthday of mine came around, my mom always had a special party for me, no matter what age I turned. She ordered or made a special cake and had all the trimmings of ice cream, chips, and punch or juice to drink. She also never failed to decorate a special room for the event with streamers, balloons, and a designated sign to commemorate the occasion. There were usually parties for every holiday, and these made us closer to each other and to all the members of our family. The real knack that Mom had, however, was making me feel so special on my date of birth, and especially thanking God for bringing me into her life. As the years progressed I thanked God too for giving me my mother, the closest person on earth to me.

Football was the celebrated sport in our family. Although I grew up watching baseball too, the former outshone this sport by a milestone. There was a historical background to this celebration, though, as my grandfather, Mom's father, had served as a football coach, as well as high school math teacher for years. He even had the given nickname, "Stoopy," because he stooped so often when he coached. The most pertinent fact concerning this occupation, however, was that Granddaddy, who was also a Golden Glove boxer at one time, had attended a football conference with Coach "Bear" Bryant of the famous collegiate Alabama Crimson Tide team. My mom said that as my grandfather spoke with Coach Bryant, he admired most Bryant's practice of allowing all team members to play at one time or another.

My grandfather recognized the fairness of this principle and adhered to it himself as much as he could, coaching the various football teams that he did during his lifetime. My granddaddy placed a high value upon treating others the way they wished to be treated, and fairness itself went hand in hand with this principle. At some point, Coach Bryant sent my mother an Alabama jacket that she treasured more than anything and wore it wherever she went and especially during those football games. She became a die-hard Bama fan for the rest of her life, but she did not leave it at that. She, in fact, spent a great deal of time converting family, friends, and even strangers to that Crimson Tide team in which she totally believed and favored.

My mom never missed a game if possible, and every single one of my little second cousins were taught to utter the words "Roll Tide Roll" upon birth or soon thereafter. She never actually got to attend a real game in person, but that did not matter because her true faithfulness to the team was often exhibited, whether it was on a game day or not. She wore her Bama sweatshirts in the winter and her Crimson Tide T-shirts during hot weather. Before it was all over and done with too, she possessed a flag, two umbrellas, jackets, sweatpants, watches, earrings, necklaces, and a backpack with *Alabama Crimson Tide* written on them. In addition, she had cups, mugs, a candle, and an actual Bear Bryant bottle of Coke, which she kept but never drank. She also had a scarf, crimson-and-white shakers, a book, and every news clipping under the sun concerning her prized team, who skyrocketed to number one often. Her blankets were adorned with this logo, and in recent years, she had her own Tide socks and a ceramic owl that my youngest second cousin painted for her in those same two colors and with the embroidered large "A" trademark of the collegiate football team.

Once as a temporary resident in a nursing rehab facility, she dressed as a Bama cheerleader for Halloween, complete with crimson-and-white pom-poms and little red bows in her hair. She even carried a roll of toilet paper in one hand, and a bottle of liquid Tide detergent in the other, with both symbolizing her two most spoken words, "Roll Tide Roll." She also consistently screamed these when she greeted anyone. I must admit too that the compliments regarding her costume were enormous in number and all over the place. Her mere presence was beaming, and everyone smiled when they saw her!

As a child, I dared not follow and support any other college team other than Bama. Like my mother, I wore shirts of crimson and white, and jewelry that reflected the same. I watched every one of those football games with her too, and we often invited my second cousin to do so also. All three of us could not wait to hold up the number-one finger when the national championship ended. My mom definitely convinced my cousin to cheer the Tide on to victory, and he still does today. I can even recall a trip to the state of Tennessee when Alabama was actually playing the Vols. After they succumbed to the Tide, Mom proudly wore her Bama shirt down the main street as I drove a Virginia-licensed car with an Alabama Crimson Tide tag neatly placed around the sides of the plate. Mom loved every minute of this, and so did I. She constantly and loudly shouted for her precious team. I enjoyed this but admit that it felt a bit embarrassing at times also.

Some of the best times that I spent with my mother were when we attended church together. As an adult, she was an outreach leader, and I often accompanied her and others on visitation days of inviting other individuals to church. She always encouraged me to attend Sunday school, children's church, and vacation Bible school on numerous occasions. I loved the singing of hymns and doing various crafts related to stories of Jesus. Mom read these stories to me too, at home, and she taught me many of the songs we sang at these events. She helped me to experience a closeness to God at an early age, for which I am grateful. At home, we always said the blessing before every meal that we shared with family. We never failed to pray at bedtime as I lay in bed before falling asleep.

With my grandmother's encouragement, Mom would lead me with "Now I lay me down to sleep. I pray the Lord my soul to keep. If I should die before I wake, I pray the Lord my soul to take." Before ending, however, they both added, "Bless us little Tillie, little Joni Walker, and little Marcclare," as my cousins and I prayed for God to be with us daily, to take care of us, and to help us do the right thing—his will—at all times. As a child, I was encouraged, as I said before, to thank God for my food and blessings before each meal. We often recited, "God is great…" My favorite prayer was this: "Thank you for the world so sweet. Thank you for the food we eat. Thank you for the birds that sing. Thank you, God, for everything." I loved this blessing so much that when I grew up and became a teacher, I taught my pupils this, and encouraged them to illustrate each phase of it when we did arts and crafts. They loved the rhymes with it too.

Christmastime was my favorite holiday, and still is, when I was a child. It was so special too, because my mom made it that way. During this time, there were a great number of family activities that we all shared together. The holiday was not complete unless we drove around town to view all the decorations that various homes in different areas offered. It was a tradition too to view the downtown Christmas lights and decor, especially what was placed upon the light poles down Main Street. I recall that one year this included a row of wreaths, and later on other decorations, such as bells, appeared there. In addition, shopping downtown at least one evening prior to Christmas was also included. I remember going to the local Woolworth store and carefully choosing candy, perfume, jewelry, or whatever I felt best suited for the person for whom I was buying.

My mom always went to another part of the store as I chose the special present that I would give to her. I remember saying also, "Don't peek, or it won't be a surprise!" She willingly complied and treasured every item that she received from me as if it were more valuable than gold. I appreciate that fact so much more now. At home we wrapped presents, of course, and on Christmas Eve we stayed in and had special holiday snacks to eat—or even Christmas cookies that we baked and decorated ourselves. The leftover ones were set out for Santa Claus, who would visit early the next morning as long as children were sound asleep. I lived with my mom and grandparents at this time, and the little Santa-face cup of coffee—which we set out for "Santa," my Granddaddy—was always empty with all the cookies gone when we woke up. Before opening presents on Christmas morning, however, we usually had a traditional breakfast of homemade coffee cake, which often included nuts and a seasoning, such as cinnamon, served warm—warm as the season of Christmas was to all our hearts.

On this day too my two cousins and I acted out the nativity scene with the following roles: I played Mary, I used one of the many dolls I had as baby Jesus, my male cousin was a proud Joseph, and his sister was always the beautiful angel who proclaimed the birth of the special one. I would drape a blue towel around my head and, solemnly, but with a smile, look at the newborn one. The whole family enjoyed singing Christmas songs, and life, I thought, was so special then. As children, we learned that Christmas was about Jesus's birth and also about giving—not necessarily presents but many things like love, support, and respect to one another. It sure was nice, however, to finally see all the toys Santa brought because we had been such good little children throughout the whole year!

I forgot to mention also that our family members loved to dress in decorative clothing on this day, including holiday-adorned sweatshirts, and sometimes we even slept in Christmas pajamas. There were so many activities at this holiday, and we enjoyed every one of them. Lastly, Mom traditionally recited, "'Twas the Night before Christmas," and it was wonderful to hear her use that deep voice of Santa Claus as he called for his reindeer to proceed in the *Rudolph the Red-Nosed Reindeer* book. She even continued this tradition with my second cousins and the little cousins who came after that. Sometimes we even got a phone call from Santa, during which Mom imitated his voice once again. We were true believers. Crucial too was the watching of the two cartoons, *Rudolph the Red-Nosed Reindeer* and *Frosty the Snowman*. Mom and I even watched these as adults every year because she simply adored them. She could not wait to tell me when they would be on television.

I remember too, as a child, speaking with her afterward about the pain of Rudolph being made fun of and Frosty's dreaded melting away in the sun. My Mom used these shows to bring forth the lessons that each presented, which totally taught me that life is not always good, but happy endings are possible, even in the midst of painful circumstances. I will never forget this lesson either, and I thank God that I was blessed with a mother who took the time to reveal this to me. With that knowledge, I have survived some pretty hard trials and tribulations. Yet I have been able to know that goodness, without a doubt, will reveal itself because that is what God promises us. Amazing! That's what my mom was too.

Later in the afternoon, my grandmother, Mamaw, always played the piano, and we all sang hymns and other songs together.

She too sang songs by herself, and we listened intently. Happily, I and my cousins, the children of the home, laughed and danced during these cherished moments. The joy that they brought will always be impressed upon my memories in my heart. It always has amazed me also that such simple activities as these could create such fun-loving and notorious remembrances in my mind.

Mom encouraged activities at home too. I will never forget owning close to forty Barbie dolls, including the hippie Ken doll and Malibu Barbie dolls, like Skipper and others. These latter ones later became known as the suntan or beach dolls with which children played. My mother's dedication to us enjoying amusement time was evident when she had a woman actually make clothes for my Barbie dolls, and she bought them constantly. I can see now in my mind the homemade, long-sleeved wedding dress with the longest and laciest train I had ever seen. There was a veil to match. Mom also made sure that I had a winter wedding gown with white fur as well as a stylish mini-dress wedding gown. I cherished each of these as my female cousin and I held beauty pageants with our collection of these dolls. Mom made sure too that these were homemade or bought at the local toy stores. I loved dolls as a little girl, and Mom surprised me with my first Barbie doll ever, Midge, who had short red hair. I simply adored her. I will always remember too that my first doll named Barbie had blond hair, while my cousin's had long brown strands. We cherished our playtimes with these just as much as those with our toy baking items that we received at Christmas. My cousin and I made numerous little cakes with my Duncan Hines play-bake oven and with her Betty Crocker play stove. The best part to us was to taste the treats when they were done.

When I was growing up, Mom allowed me to participate in numerous other activities. I was a Brownie Scout, a Girl Scout, a Pee Wee football cheerleader, and a baton twirler. With the first two, I earned many badges, like cooking and sewing, but also had fun doing things, such as roasting marshmallows over a campfire and decorating a float for a local holiday parade. With the latter, I learned to make tissue paper flowers in Girl Scout colors of green and gold and place them on the float.

When I was a cheerleader, Mom made sure that I had a red, white, and blue uniform for games in the winter and another one for those during warm nights, I wore a red skirt and a white sweater with a big blue *N* sewn on it to name our North Pewee football team. The other uniform consisted of a one-piece red dress-like outfit, also with a blue *N* and complete with white bobby socks and hair clips or bows of the same color. Mom also set me up with baton-twirling lessons, and I became a majorette with red spangled costumes and multi-colored other ones. Mom also bought me a cross section of batons, each in a category of its own. Initially, I twirled a plain one. Then, I became the proud owner of a baton whose ends could change colors to match my costumes, a large gray steel hoop baton, and finally, a fire one. I never did much with the latter before my interest in any lessons diminished.

Mom was proud of me when I entered various contests, and I even won some medals and trophies to place on high shelves in my bedroom for display. I was proud of these honors too, although I was often nervous and scared to perform in front of groups of people. I managed to do exactly that, though, and learned to be calmer the more I progressed to different types of shows. I was so thankful to my mother for giving me each of these experiences that allowed me to meet people and do various things, like marching in parades, which brought me sheer joy.

Aside from these activities, as a child I remember attending movies at our downtown local theaters, and later, at the showplace at the city mall. Mom allowed me to go to proper movies, like those by Walt Disney, and often popular shows of the day that she deemed appropriate. I do not remember much, but I was always told by her that my first movie attended was, of course, *Bambi*. I sincerely believe that my love for deer and my views of them as peaceful creatures resulted from this attendance. I also recall watching *Sleeping Beauty* and *Snow White and the Seven Dwarfs*. When I grew older, Mom also gave permission to me to see shows such as *The Swiss Family Robinson*. My male first cousin and I were so impressed by its theme that we went straight home to my grandparents' house to build, of all things, our own house in a tree. I remember too that we did not succeed too well in doing so because that task was more difficult than expected. I do remember that it was still fun trying, though.

Mom also took me to the lion movie *Born Free*. I cried during portions, but Mom comforted me with hugs, and as usual we discussed the sad parts together. When we were kids and went to a particular show, my mom, my aunt, or my grandmother would always pack us a delicious snack to hide in a purse or bag since we were really not to sneak anything in with us. Food prices at the theater were extreme then, just as they are now, and this was our solution to keeping costs down.

I believe that my entire family sat together to watch the premiere of *Cinderella*, not the cartoon, on the television set in my grandparents' living room. That show made me joyful and sad at once. I remember smiling when the truth of who really wore the glass slipper was revealed. Even Sundays became a family day each weekend. On it, we all had a big meal, seated around a big kitchen table after church services. This meal was often juicy pot roast, complete with carrots, potatoes, and onions. We also conversed and sang around the piano on this day. While seated at the eating table, my cousins and I could not resist playing silent games with our relatives. For example, with a glance to one another and a slight pointing at each other's drinks, we began our "See Who Drinks Last" game. Then we watched carefully as each adult sipped from the lunch cups, and when the last one had done so, we congratulated him as the winner. Silly as it seemed, we always had fun with this activity.

We also enjoyed making up the "Cake Batter" game with every bowl of ice cream that we received for dessert. This activity involved stirring our ice cream until we felt the "batter" was smooth enough to eat. We constantly asked aloud, "Is it ready yet?" With each negative response, we stirred and stirred until there were no lumps in the bowl, and joyfully we ate it all with the biggest smiles upon our faces. I am grateful that my mom, my aunt, and my grandparents never dismissed these little creative kid games held religiously at the table during a meal. I am glad that they saw no harm in our activities as long as we did what we were supposed to do—eat and use good table manners. I believe that these little activities enhanced our imagination and creative talents as well as aided us in growing up comfortably with attaining a good freedom of expression.

At Halloween time, as a young girl, I favored the following three dress-up costumes: a bride, a hula girl, and a princess. I am pretty sure that my love for my mother deeply affected my choices of outfits for trick-or-treating. I adored being dressed as a girl about to be married because I perceived my mother, my favorite role model in the world, as being such a beautiful one before I came along. When Mom purchased a long brown-haired wig for whatever reasons, I snatched it up to wear and dress up as a Hawaiian girl, complete with a beautiful red flower in my long strands. I remember that my mom bought me a grass skirt, flip-flops, and a floral bathing suit top that matched my hair flower perfectly. Since Mom allowed me to take baton-twirling lessons, I had all sorts of tiaras and crowns that she got for me to wear during various events. I loved the whole silver crown that she neatly pinned on top of my head as I wore a pink or white long dress to become a true princess for Halloween one year. I remember her putting some of her rosy red lipstick on me and telling me how beautiful it made me look. The predominant thought in my little mind at that time was that I hopefully looked as beautiful as my loving Mom always did and that I would, of course, get lots and lots of Halloween candy.

In my mother's later years, also my years as an adult, we remained close in relationship to one another. In fact, I cannot thank my mom enough for her special assistance when I grew up and got jobs of my own. My occupations, too included teaching and directing, along with the tasks associated with these jobs. My loving mother graciously served as a substitute when regular teachers were out. This helped me immensely. She made countless trips to the store with me for school supplies and day care supplies, like 100 percent juice (sometimes twenty-five cans at a time), snacks (containing vitamin A), and many materials for arts and crafts. Mom also carried every bag of these items with me into whatever educational environment they belonged. She even helped me cover cots with sheets for nap time, and almost every weekend we visited my work site just to get things in order for the next week! Precious and gracious she was to me, and I probably never thanked her enough. If she ever grew tired of or annoyed by any of this, she pursued on helping her daughter to do the best job possible and whatever it entailed.

I remember too various trips that we took "to get away from it all" to the Smokey Mountains. We loved shopping and eating there. We never failed to take in a show at one of the theaters that offered singing and dancing. In the motel room Mom loved the songs of the fifties best. Each trip too, back then, I, being a teacher, loved it when Mom helped me to pick out a special gift—including home-made candy or a holiday decoration—for my entire group of little students. We particularly enjoyed browsing through the Christmas and gospel stores. The lights, the decorations, and the scents of pine and evergreen made us happy and excited about the holiday to come, even if we were shopping in the fall or spring. We also adored the sense of peace that the atmosphere of the gospel stores gave to us. Here too we were able to view spiritual materials, like bookmarks and unique items that reminded us of spending time with God.

It was also sheer joy and pure fun to walk down the streets and see the variety of the activities, such as candle making, taking place. I even collected dolls at that time, and a favorite store, Dolls by Candlelight, was where I purchased a brunette doll with a long red dress and named her Walker, from my middle name. Mom was so pleased! She loved that name. We also enjoyed the outdoors, live concerts where local performers showed off their talents to passersby. Sometimes Mom and I would dance and sing along. I have to admit that her bold personality often made me shy but super thrilled that she delighted so much in all the entertainment. We also toured the candy stores, and fudge was always on our list to buy. We enjoyed eating it right away or in the motel room where we rested until our next excursion occurred. This too included a ride on the sky lift and, once, a trip up the Space Needle where we could view everything.

This Space Needle trip was a bit scary, however, when Mom vowed to never ride it again. Initially, we had to take an elevator up the needle. On another day after the experience, Mom glanced at it again and claimed, "That thing is swaying in the wind," as she stood on the ground level of the sidewalk. I do not know if it was really moving or not. Yet when she said it, I was certain that I detected the Needle going back and forth. This scared me enough to vow also to never take a ride up and down it again. I will cherish all these memories in my heart forever because our bond—Mom's and mine—grew even stronger and larger then, if that is even possible.

As adults, Mom and I both loved to share special times with my first cousin's children. She had three boys and one girl. We truly enjoyed taking them to McDonald's or simply out for ice cream. We also shared movies with them, and they had many overnighters with us at our house. One of our most enjoyable times was when we took them to two live performances at the local venue for such events. First of all, Barney, the purple dinosaur, made a visit to our town. As he sang and danced on a multicolored stage filled with tall rainbow flowers, pink and red lollipops, and colorful pictures of everything, we watched the smiles of and listened to the shrieks of our little relatives as they consistently sang to songs, such as "I Love You, You Love Me." They simultaneously learned rhymes, the alphabet, and colors. During another year, Dora the Explorer appeared in a show at the same venue. Each one of us waved little Dora flags, given to us at the door, as the main character presented a program. Dora's Map led her and her friends to a special place or treasure. One of Mom's and my favorite parts of the night was speaking Spanish with our little kin people during the ride home. We said words like *bueno* for *good* and *hola* for *hi* or *hello*.

Toward the latter years of Mom's life, our lives together were happy but quieter than previous years. We were both unable to work, and the quietness was unfortunately because of a series of health-related problems for both of us. Mom was always there when I needed her, and vice versa. Need her I did when each of the following situations occurred. I had my first kidney stone, and my mother stood by my side through all the pain and problems that that event brought. Having experienced four more later, I likewise had her, and she waited on me for every need that arose. I loved that. When a baby-sized tumor developed on my right ovary, and I was forced to have my first surgery, she was there too. During months of recovery and a grand diagnosis of "no cancer," she cooked me some of the best meals ever, she took long walks with me outside to help me build up my strength, and she went to every single medical appointment with me before and after the operation too.

She dried my tears of frustration while she celebrated the days of joy when full recovery was near. She uttered words of encouragement to me daily, like, "You can do this with God's help," and I can vividly see her praying for me, even in the middle of a television show we were watching. I saw her lips moving at that time. I, a bit concerned, asked boldly, "What are you doing, Mom?" "Praying," she softly answered each time. Without her prayers and presence, without her staunch dedication to me, and without her love for me, I never would have healed. She often reminded me of God's role in this too.

Mom also stood strongly by my side during two other health issues. I had always prided myself with the fact that I had never broken a bone of any type in my life. Yet one day, while trying to separate our little kitten from our big dog, I fell over the coffee table in our living room and broke my ankle. This was a very difficult time for me, and I often felt that I was never going to walk properly again. My dedicated Mom helped me to do this, along with physical therapy. She went almost everywhere with me as I wore a red-and-white "candy cane" brace-like cast as it was the month of December. Strangely enough too, at another point, I had a huge tear in my shoulder, and she stood by me through tedious orthopedic appointments as well as the surgery to repair it. The surgeon, who was great, gave Mom pictures of the procedure itself, and she loved to explain the mending process to whoever would listen. Mom and I both shared with everyone that the doctor actually took a piece of my collarbone to repair it. We were both amazed by this! We were both glad when my shoulder healed because I never realized, nor did she, how much assistance I would need with minor tasks, like brushing my teeth, combing my hair, and even eating food. Mom helped me to accomplish all these, though.

I stayed by my mother's side throughout her later life too. On a job site, she fell, breaking both her knee and her wrist on the same side at the same time. She utilized a platform walker, and she stayed at my apartment during the entire recovery process and during the physical therapy trips. I had a full-time job then, teaching as well as directing, and it was an extremely difficult experience for both of us. Two parts of the body needed to heal, and after a certain amount of time, they did. I will never forget either that my mother went back to work then and at another job, though ordered by her doctor to not have a standing-on-her-feet job. She did so anyway. Her response to questioning concerning this was simply, "I need to do this for us. It will be fine." When I pondered this over and over again, I realized more than ever that this is what you do when you love someone. You sacrifice.

After two serious falls, my mother had two stays in two different nursing home and rehabilitation facilities. I always claimed, "I will never put my mother in a nursing home," but both of these situations were "have to" cases for her and for me both. My mother adored being home with me as much as I adored being there with her. We loved to watch movies and television shows. She and I also took pure delight in just watching the change of seasons in the house in which we lived together.

There is a big picture window in the living room, and in the wintertime we loved to watch the snowflakes come down. In warm times, we sat on our screened-in porch and had some of the best conversations concerning anything and also appreciated how pretty the flowers in the yard were. We loved watching the various birds fly through our trees. Sparrows, robins, cardinals, blue jays, and even a hummingbird nested somewhere near our house, and we watched some of them feed their young babies. I know that life has so much more meaning when you stop to observe the miracles—even everyday ones—that God has created for all of us. The smile on my mother's face during these times was reward enough for me, and I will never forget how much she loved the screened-in porch. I miss those times too that we shared meals together in that very spot. We enjoyed these tremendously.

Sometimes during and in between nursing home stays, my mom encountered two more complications. Going to an appointment, she actually fell on one of the facility's parking lots and regrettably broke her ankle. This happened only a few days prior to her release to come home. This delayed her trip home several months, but sometime right after Christmas, she did come, and we celebrated the holiday a bit late, but celebrate we did. Our best present that year was being together at our home, surrounded by a beautifully decorated Christmas tree with blue-and-white lights and an Alabama Crimson Tide snowman, fully dressed in winter clothing and proudly sitting on the mantel in our living room. I was actually surprised more than once at the courage and strength that she always found to recover from what she endured.

Unfortunately, and sometime later, Mom actually swallowed a chicken bone when she was having dinner. Unbelievable to me and to her, this perforated her esophagus, and the bone itself lodged in the side of her neck. After a painful endoscopy showed that the piece was not down in the throat area, an immediate surgery took place. I was told by the doctor too that my precious mother might not make it. I could hardly believe the circumstances in which I found myself; I sat in the lobby of a local hospital, part of the time with a friend, talking about the funny things that my mom had done throughout her life. The friend and I prayed, and for a very long time, my mother remained in the operating room. I sat alone for the rest of the hours, and if I remember correctly, the total time was six solid ones. I cried profusely; I feared the worst, and I could not imagine life without my loving parent. I realized, at one point, that I was not really alone though. As I prayed incessantly, I felt God's presence with me.

By this time, the lights had dimmed somewhat in the lobby where I sat, and even hospital workers for the day in that particular area had departed. It was dim, but I was not totally alone. After a period of what seemed like a lifetime to me, the doctor came into the area and described, in full detail, that she was in intensive care and was also on a ventilator. When I finally walked into my mother's hospital room, fear temporarily enveloped me, and I was so glad to see her that I burst into tears. She could only nod to answer me, but something remarkable happened. The timing of this event, first of all, occurred during the weekend that Alabama was playing Tennessee for the yearly college match. I kid you not when I describe my mother's first gestures, not actual words, then. Unexpectedly but fantastically, she rolled both arms and hands in a circling motion and then spread both out on each side. I was actually able to decipher this without any assistance at all. All the motions simply signified these two words: "Roll Tide." My first reaction was to laugh aloud and then very happily and as noisily I could, I said, "She's going to be fine," and she was. Thank God!

In this chapter, I have given both my childhood as well as adulthood backgrounds regarding me and my mother. I discussed both of these because I want the reader of this book to know what our lives were like prior to her unexpected death. I also want to share the closeness and love that we experienced with one another. Such information is pertinent prior to reading the next chapter's events because these descriptions here depict the actual facts about how we were and what things were really like between us. It must be explained too that ours, like anyone else's existence, was not perfect. No one's is but God's. In other words, we sometimes had arguments with one another, as well as disagreements, of course. But that's life! This chapter merely catalogs some of the journey of our lives. The most significant thing that I, as a writer, can convey to everyone is simply this: I loved my mother more than anything, and neither one of us would ever harm one another in any way, shape, or form. That is the truth regarding this whole situation! Lastly and proudly, I wish to say that our lives were so intertwined that each of our main concerns included those for one another. Nothing can change that, thank God. Our relationship was enduring, and we were close all of our lives together. For me alone, that was fifty-seven years! I grew up, stayed in the same town, and, fortunately, stayed close to my mother all her life—a life that ended so quickly on earth to me. Not too many children and parents have that claim, but we did.

CHAPTER TWO

# The Actual Events

Even though I walk through the valley of the shadow
of death, I fear no evil, for you are with me…
—Psalm 23:4

It was a cold winter morning, December 29, 2018. Our family was extremely excited because the day before, the twenty-eighth, my second cousin had just given birth to her second child, and it was a little girl! A few days earlier, our family members had celebrated Christmas Eve together at my house, still minus those key members—my grandparents, my aunt, and my first cousin. The last two had died young and so unexpectedly. My mother and I had had a special holiday of our own on Christmas Day, eating holiday foods opening gifts, and simply spending time together. It was really nice. We loved holiday time better than any other—even though things had changed somewhat a great deal, with the losses of so many key figures in our clan. We knew that this Christmas would be extra special because of the birth of a new child in our family, plus it was going to be a girl!

I thought about how I first found out the gender. My second cousin gave me a sealed envelope after my promise not to open it until I dropped her off at work from the doctor appointment. She did not want to know herself. The reason for this secret was her plan that afternoon to have a "gender reveal" party with her little preschool-age son, her husband, and a close girlfriend with whom she had gone to school. My cousin had bought pink and blue Silly

Strings for her friend's mother to announce the blessed event, correct color and all. I was just sincerely thrilled that day that she so trusted me to find out first. We had been close since her mother's death a few years earlier. As soon as my second cousin left my car, I quickly tore open the sealed medical envelope. It was just as I had expected and had actually hoped at that time. I smiled and thought, *It's a girl!* I felt like I was smiling on the outside as well as the inside. I was thrilled that there would be a female cousin in addition to the male one already present. After opening the envelope myself, I remember being so excited to the point that I could barely control my emotions in front of my mother, who was waiting patiently at home to hear the news.

Mom was just as happy as I was when she heard. Her beautiful smile revealed that affirmatively. She, I, and other family members already knew too that labor was to be induced on December 28. During that inducement, too, my second cousin's little three-year-old was going to stay with Mom and me while the whole event occurred. Her little boy was excited—ecstatic to be exact! I think we all worried a little bit about how he would handle being away from his parents overnight for the first time. His mother had carefully explained the scenario to him in advance, and he was fine with it! In fact, he loved Mom and me dearly, and our feelings for him were mutual. He had spent plenty of time with us before, though never all night. Mom and I were looking so forward to it, and I, having been a teacher of young kids, readied myself as if it were a precious job for me.

I gathered up all the holiday crafts I could, including Christmas stickers of stockings, bells, snowmen, and angels. I found green paper trees and shiny decorations to glue on them. I even went to a local dollar store to find stained glass objects to paint and other red and green items to make. I also purchased red-and-white pipe cleaners to create candy canes. It helped a great deal too when his mother brought an enormous bag of leftover holiday crafts from her own class for us to use. When she told me about it, I kept earnestly reminding her not to forget to bring it because, I said, "I want us to have as many things to do as is possible."

As I bought each of the items, I thought about what a darling little boy he was with his thick dark hair and his grand dark eyes. In fact, he was honestly the most beautiful baby I had ever seen. He and I simply clicked with one another. That meant that we were so perfect together. We could not have adored each other and each other's company more. We read together, did crafts together, and talked together nonstop. Much of this had taken place in the past when he had spent time with us. My mother enjoyed our interaction more than anything. She constantly told me that she could see how much he idolized me every time we came together. I knew she was right too, and only God knows the true joy that being with that little boy gave me. I taught him numerous songs, and he truly had perfect pitch when he sang—a gift he received from his talented mother, no doubt! My favorite thing was when we laughed wholeheartedly together. I could always see his beautiful brown eyes smile then also, and this was wonderful. Mom and I were both thrilled that she chose us to be his buddies at this significant time in all our lives.

On the morning of December 29, one day after our newest family member had come into this world, my little cousin, my mom, and I were sleeping in the living room of our residence. It was a cold day, but we were all wrapped up warmly in winter blankets. We had chosen to sleep in this room because we could all be close to one another and to the television set. Everything had been busy but fine that day, and I remember being really exhausted after taking care of Mom, my little cousin, all our pets and activities of the day. I looked forward for the rest to come. Not once did I expect the scenario to be! As we were all resting, I was awakened suddenly and shockingly by the piercing screams of my elderly mother. It was not unusual for her to ask for something during the middle of the night because she needed help with her walker should she need to get up from her chair. Yet when I heard the loudness of her voice, I could not help but feel that something was terribly wrong.

Before hearing her say twice, "I can't breathe," I managed to glance at the clock situated on our living room mantel. Mom had asked me to put it there since we never had a timepiece in that room of the house until recently. She spent most of her moments here, and to put it there was the perfect idea. It was almost four thirty in the morning. In a matter of seconds, I jumped up and ran over to my mother's side, demanding, "What's the matter, Mom?" She kept her eyes closed, and then I asked, "Can't you breathe?"

She shook her head no, took one more breath, and did not move. I had been trained numerous times in CPR as a teacher, and my gut reaction was to attempt chest compressions. When they did not seem to work, my whole demeanor changed. I believe I became in a state of shock. I now know it was a state of extreme denial. My attention was suddenly drawn to my little cousin who awoke, apparently, when his great aunt exclaimed her inability to breathe. At that moment, I remember him saying, "Rosey"—that was what he called her—"is singing a song." Much later, I reviewed his words, thinking that as a preschooler, he must have likened her repetition of not being able to breathe to the singing of a chime or song. Having taught, I knew that his age group learned things through repetition. This was what I thought had happened. I do not remember responding to his words, but I tried to smile at him to let him know I heard him. When my mother breathed a last breath, he remarkably said, "Now she is asleep." In my state of uncertainty and shock then, I remember saying, for whatever reason, "Yes, she is," to him quietly. The details following all this are very foggy for me, but I do recall taking my small cousin as soon as possible to the hospital to be with his parents and new baby sister. I do, however, know that my little cousin told my mother "Bye" as he always did, and he may even have said that he loved her. This was his regular routine when he left our house.

As I consider all these events now, these details seem so short and simple at this moment. I do not belittle the extreme truth of them when I say this. What I mean is that in an odd way, there was peacefulness, to some degree, as it all transpired. I do not believe now that for my mom, there existed any overbearing pain or suffering. I need to believe this too if I can ever have any form of tranquility or acceptance of any kind myself. I see it now as having taken place in a split second. I know currently also that the aftermath of the circumstances was anything but serene. I found out that its twists and turns were so complicated that their presence seems to forever exist in a circle of uncertainty and shame for me. Unexpected too was my reaction to the situation as well as inexplicable to society and especially to me. Strangely enough also. I carried them out.

CHAPTER THREE

# A State of Denial

Do not worry about tomorrow for tomorrow will bring
worries of its own. Today's trouble is enough for today.
—Matthew 6:34

If asked what happened next, I would sincerely respond that that
is the question of the century for me. I know too that the answer
is varied, complicated, and void of some details. I believe also
that the response might even be, "Everything that possibly could
took place." I define that as anything that could take place did, and
so did more than that!

I cannot honestly remember many of the events that took place
after my December 29 trip to the local hospital. At this point, I began
to not really reason or decipher clearly the situation anymore. Only
one thought then overrode any others in my mind. I totally blocked
somehow the entire morning's occurrences. I simply thought that
they never happened. Instead, I went into a mode of what I now call
autopilot. I describe this best as doing automatically what I would
normally do as if no change had taken place at all in my life. I did not
cry. I did not grieve. I did not notify anyone because in my thoughts
and beliefs, there was no reason to do so. Did I snap in my mind to
a state of refusal to accept that anything was wrong? I do not actually know, but I can only think that something such as this is what
happened. I cannot explain it in any other way. I find it difficult to
conceive also. I somehow continued my life as if everything was the
same as the prior day's happenings.

If anyone asked about me, I would answer that all was fine with me. I did not act out of the ordinary initially toward anyone, as far as my knowledge is concerned. I came into contact with family, friends, and strangers at that time. I managed to continue doing the usual things that I did daily. For example, I drove my youthful cousins to various places, as I had continually done since their mother's unexpected passing a few years earlier. I took one of them to her work site as well as to medical appointments. Some of those doctor appointments were for her children also, including the new baby. I even transported her to a college campus for classes and kept the new child for short periods of time then. I also gave rides to her youngest brother to school and sport practices. I took care of home matters, although I hesitate to evaluate my performances with these, such as pet care.

I say this now because I do not, as I said before, remember all events during this time. I do recall making some trips to the grocery store for items needed. I shopped for friends and had conversations with them. I remember eating some of the time but rarely sleeping. I am certain of one thing: I never left the premises of my house overnight. I spent every single night at my residence until other matters transpired in time and which are discussed in the appropriate chapter of this book. When I left during the day temporarily, I can remember one other action I took for certain and possibly each time. I told my mother that I loved her and gently pat her bed covers as I uttered these words. I often said, "I'll be back soon, Mom," or "I'll be back as quickly as I can," when I departed too.

During this entire time, I solely believed that nothing had happened to my mother. In other words, she was not gone from this world. I could never let my mind go to a place of losing the most precious person to me. I was incapable of doing so. I sincerely think that unacceptance of reality was easier than the alternative of acceptance.

I attribute each of my actions as well as failures to act to the closeness of our relationship together. With respect to a long period of time, we shared all our lives for exactly that—all our lives. I know too that we did have lives of our own. Yet we always kept each other informed of one another's living though. In many ways too, even when I was an adult, my mother was very overprotective of me. I realize currently that she never wanted me to get hurt. She loved me that much. I also realize that she did the best by me that she could. Did it start with me almost drowning in a pool during a Florida vacation? Was she hurt in life and wanted me to never experience that pain also? I do not know, but I can remember her constantly worrying about me when we were not physically with one another. In my mind too, I sometimes felt that she never wanted me to leave her.

When I had to go somewhere, she always concerned herself with my safety—and even the safety of other family members—to the point that she would worry if none of us came back when she thought we should. Sometimes I found her caring too much a little overpowering, but I was so glad that I had a mother who really cared. I often thought that some unfortunate children do not have that blessing. I was also relieved we had one another. Numerous phone calls came to me when we were apart—actually too many to count. Often before I left the driveway, she would call and say, "Hurry back!" I was calm and simply assured her that I would do exactly what she asked. I proceeded to go to whatever destination I had and actually waited for her next call. It came pretty soon too, and a great deal of repeating my plans and words to return ASAP followed. Mom always sounded concerned when she called—almost as if she feared that something would tear me away from her permanently. I reassured her as much as I could. Then I continued going wherever I was going—to the store, to an appointment, or whatever. I never felt that the worst was to come. I quite frankly wanted to return when I was able and view her at peace with my presence once again.

I never asked my mother, "What would you do if I died, Mom?" I couldn't because I had seen enough of the fear and worry that she already had if I was gone only a few minutes. She never told me what to do either if I suddenly found myself alone, without her to parent, love, and stand by my side. In my mind, I never went there extremely, but only to feel that if she were gone, I would want to be gone too. That was all there was to it. This was my solution to that situation. I guess Mom's feelings regarding my presence were made with those nervous phone calls when I would have to go somewhere. Yet we never, face-to-face, discussed either what her life would be like without mine. I sense now, more than ever, that she must have considered this with all her exceptional worrying, but I never approached that subject with her beyond my constant promises to return to her from wherever I traveled.

I realize now, especially that this was all abnormal-unusual to say the least. As I read my own words now depicting my reactions, it sounds unreal and even crazy to me. More importantly, however, this entire scenario seems very sad and desperate. I know that Mom and I loved one another and were closer to each other than anyone I've ever known. I believe that neither one of us could imagine life without the other. I think too that Mom, perhaps, hinted at my absence with all her constant anxiety and on more than one occasion. I, on the other hand, could never face any thoughts such as that because it was too extreme a thing with which to deal.

As I write about these events of denial too, I never realized how many days had passed since the December 29 morning activities. I was informed later that forty-four days was the actual number. My so-called days of normalcy were not really that at all. I refrained from accepting that my mother was not alive all this time. A headline in some newspaper gave me the actual amount of days.

In summary for me, all this will be like a stain in a piece of clothing that is incapable of ever being removed. It will never go away—go away from my record or my life. My satisfaction is that I did not harm anyone, and I did not kill anyone, though I felt later that many people thought so. I was incapable of telling anybody. I could not call 911 or emergency personnel because of the shock, and later denial, of the actual event. I told myself that she was not gone, and remarkably and negatively—to all of us—I lived or survived accordingly. I had no concept of time then. I was almost like a robot that performed what was expected, with no feelings regarding what had actually taken place.

I have always been an emotional person. During other times in my life, I have never been able to control my feelings, especially when I have been sad, scared, unsure, or subject to unexpected change. Everyone who knows me knows this about me. I've never been able to hide my emotions because they are always there for all to see. Her actual death could not be real to me because of the devastating origin of events and because of my firm denial of it. Why do I personally believe all this took place? I do not have all the answers, but now I do think it was too shocking and way too difficult for me to grasp. We physically lived with one another most of our lives. We took care of one another. We loved each other too. I could not accept that she would ever leave me, even though reality tells me that this is a part of life. I blocked the truth of what I never wanted to be a part.

I cannot explain completely what I went through because I still do not comprehend all of it myself. I recognize that labels, such as "horrifying," "unusual," and "unascertainable," have been utilized to describe my story. I agree with these descriptions—and many others. I am not currently proud of any of this situation, nor will I ever be. I honestly do not know how I lived through any of it. I believe that I will have to live with it for the rest of my life. Coupled with attempting to cope with Mom's death itself, this all is more than overwhelming. It is hardly understandable, even to me. I cannot believe either that for the rest of my life, no matter what, it will always be a part of what took place during my existence. Even if I wanted to escape it—and believe me, I have—I cannot. It is worse with which to deal too, because I have always tried—100 percent—to do the right thing. Finding out later that I broke a law—the one involving the concealment of a body—was more than a shock to me. Not one single time did it enter my mind to go against the legal system. I was not aware of such a law in the first place. I am certain that ignorance is no excuse either. Yet I have not forgotten that I denied her passing. In my opinion, it is extremely difficult to deliberately hide a body when an individual denies, in a state of shock, that there was a death in the first place. I explain this more in a later chapter of this book.

# CHAPTER FOUR

# Two Oddities

If your sons are careful of their way, to walk before me
in truth, with all their heart and with all their soul,
you shall not lack a man on the throne of Israel.

—1 Kings 2:4

I do know that this situation already has numerous peculiar or out-of-the-ordinary happenings associated with it. I must tell about two more oddities that are parts of the story also. Two other parts of my actions did take place, and to this day are somewhat inexplicable to me and probably to most of the world aware of this incidence. First of all, I performed an action, at that time, that stood out in the minds of society as well as in my own. I covered my mom with a tremendous number of blankets—even clothing—and this activity was more than noted in every form of media that exists in our world today. I began doing this sometime after the morning events of December 29, which took place at my home. I cannot say exactly when any of this occurred because I do not honestly remember. I just know it happened during the time that I failed to accept the passing of my mother, who meant everything to me. I also cannot explain why this reaction took place. I do recall never removing any of the so-called covers as I placed more on top of the ones already there. Do I find this activity strange as I go over it again and again in my mind? Of course I do, as well as think that everything done at that moment in my life was. One theory, presented to me, suggests that I placed these since I cared for my mother on a daily basis—often changing the linens and blankets that she utilized. I cannot answer to this though either. I only know that I refrained from accepting that she was no longer alive, along with this abnormal reaction.

On a second basis, I realize that many questions were posed by others regarding the smell or odor in my house during the extended time that passed. I know that this refers to the actual decomposition of my mother's body. People have asked me if I watched her physical being decompose in front of my very eyes. I answer definitely, no. I could never do that with regard to anyone, especially my mother whose life's ending I could never grasp in the first place. I want everyone to know that the thought of decomposition never entered my mind during this entire situation. I am the kind of person who finds that subject uncertain and scary, among other highly negative and dismal terminology. Because of its origin, I have never brought my mind to think about it, even then.

Many individuals asked me also about the smell or odor in my home when my mother's body—not recognized by me as a body— was present. I do not have the clear-cut, or even expected, answers to these interrogations either. I only know what I do remember during the time. There was a smell, or I never would have purchased all the deodorizers. I clearly remember that the only question that the detective had was if I bought them all at the same time at the same store. I responded that they were purchased at different times at different stores because I do recall doing that. I later saw a police report that claimed that I masked the smell of Mom's body with all the air fresheners. I never said that. A question concerning this was never asked to me. Therefore, I do not deny detecting an odor, but during the time I did refuse to accept that my mom was deceased. I did smell something, but I believed whatever it was would go away if I used the deodorizers. Reality was, it would not. I can further declare that I must have blocked the intensity of the smell for the simple reason that I stayed there the whole time with the few exceptions of going to a few places, but once again was never gone all night. I was stunned when an individual told me that the extreme odor of decomposition or mummification was so strong, even after a few days. This discovery alone made me question over and over again how I did what I did. Yet I have no solution. Lastly, I do recognize that my first sensation of an intolerable stench was February 11, 2019, and the details surrounding this are in the next chapter of this book.

CHAPTER FIVE

# Reality Sets In

Jesus Wept.
—John 11:35

Reality for me again began to set in on Monday, February 11, 2019. Before describing this actual day, however, I want to state that I, prior to this time, continued to live my life as if my mother were still alive—denying the aspects of her death over and over again. As explained in the previous chapters, I continued normal activities too, and for approximately a month, my own family failed to notice anything out of the ordinary. These individuals did not always visit us unless there was a special day, such as a family birthday, and during this time these were nonexistent. I know too that the deaths of key members of our family sometimes change a certain way or traditions that used to be when everyone was still around. I took care of my mother daily, and no one else assisted me a great deal prior to her death. When the time did come that questions were asked, I, still in denial, reverted to a tactic that I never utilized where Mom was concerned.

I did get physically sick myself several times, and this was a true excuse for no one to visit, should there be any requests. I then simply told myself that Mom was ill too. This idea was so much easier for me to believe than any other alternative, such as death. I told my counselor, who knows the truth about me completely, that we were both ill—Mom and I. Then I had reasons to miss any appointments set during this time of events. I not only astonished her when the truth was revealed; I shocked myself also. When she asked me about this later, I had been unable, because of the shock and denial, to conceive of the time gone by then—much less of all the appointments missed. I know also that, before the tragic death of my mom, I always went to every appointment with my counselor because each one was significant to me and helped me to deal with the negative issues in my life. A great number of those existed too. Therefore, I had no true comprehension of any of this until actual reality set in.

The happenings then on Monday, February 11, 2019, were truthfully the opposite of uncertainty, denial, and inability to recognize some facts in my actual life. This date was ironically a few days before Saint Valentine's Day, a holiday my mother and I loved to share together. In fact, celebrating any holiday together was always special for us because we could spend it together as family, as best friends, and as two individuals who had an exceptional bond with one another. I always knew too that this connection between mother and child was incomparable to any other in my life. I never wanted to see it broken on this earth either. I even discovered later—later than February 11—that I actually put up a few pieces of Valentine's Day decor, but I cannot honestly remember doing that. I saw the decorations when I came back to the house after my mother's body was found. I cried when I took them down finally. The reason for my tears was because this was the first time I did not remember decorating my home for a special holiday. I also decorated during these times for myself, but mostly for my mom since she enjoyed and loved every piece of decor so much. Doing this gave me purpose in life when I was no longer working as a teacher. With that career absent, so were the brightly colored seasonal items of decoration and fun that I had in my classroom. I found it enjoyable to dress up my home instead. It gave me the joy and satisfaction that Mom had with regard to this.

My February 11 thoughts and perceptions were totally negative in nature. I believe that several events, including my first detection of the actual overwhelming smell in my house, prompted my mind to revert from denial to several realizations at this time. In fact, this stench, which had never really gotten to me, overwhelmed me—on the morning of February 11—to the point that I threw up several times. I suddenly became scared and extremely sad. I then experienced a panic attack. I had not had one of these in a long time. Afterward, a strong sense of desperation and hopelessness took over my whole being. I had numerous thoughts of suicide, and at a certain point, the smell overtook me again, and all I could think about was leaving the premises and never coming back. I was ready to go, and then I remembered my pets. I realized that they must be fed, and I put out extra amounts of food for them because of my planned non-return. Then huge guilty feelings made me think twice about leaving my beloved dog to which I had always been close. She was more like a human than an animal to me. She also loved me unconditionally. I loved my cats just as much, but felt they had each other and would do better in my absence than my pooch would. That tremendous guilt impressed me so much that I could not imagine leaving her behind.

My mode of transportation then was a van, which became the replacement when transmission problems befell my car. I mention this fact too, because it became significant since getting up in a van—higher off the ground, of course—was more difficult for the dog to do than I expected. Oddly enough too, she had never ridden in this vehicle since I got it. These details surrounding my dog may seem petty, but I hold my pets very close to my heart. I love them dearly, and they are important to me and to my life. I thought, during this time, that my mother had always encouraged me to treat them as family members because she said, "That's who they are." I knew also that my mind had reverted to reality since I recognized these actual feelings and the words that my mom used often. I suddenly screamed aloud and was totally absorbed in extreme grief, which I had not experienced at any time during this entire situation. I cried for a long time.

The picture in my mind then was of my mother taking her last breath. I had not allowed my mind to accept that image before now either. "O my God," I said, "she is really gone." I could not bear to look at the recliner in which I now would see my mother lifeless. All this was so unbearable to me at this exact moment. I have never felt the way I did then in my life. This was my precious mother—the sole person in my world who had always been in my world. At this time, I knew that the only way I could deal with this was simply not deal with it at all. I wanted to die. Before getting into my van myself, I felt the need to explain the circumstances of her death, to express gratitude to those dear to me, and to even direct, in a written note, to whom the contents of my house would go. I took paper and pen to my front porch, sat down, and with many tears wrote these messages on three separate pieces of notebook paper—

a note explaining that my mother died peacefully on December 29, 2018, at four thirty in the morning. On this paper too, I wrote, "I died the day that she died." A second piece of paper was a brief note of gratitude to some really good friends. Lastly, in a third note, I made it known that all the possessions in my home were to be left to my remaining family members. As I stated, I felt the need to do this, and I left the writings to be found by someone who would come to my house. After doing this, I and my dog left. Reality had set in, without a doubt, even though it was really horrifying for me to finally accept, and I had chosen not to do so before now. This was to say, at the very least, a nightmare.

I headed out then to an unknown destination with a specific plan—a plan to end my life on this earth. In my mind, the reality of this was certain, but the details were not. Therefore, three definite questions also raced through my brain. These included: "Where do I go?" "How do I carry out my final plan?" and "What happens to my dog at this time?" I had actually taken bottles of medication with me. I had even narrowed down the methods of killing myself to two—an overdose or driving over a cliff. I really concerned myself—as far as worry goes—with my dog more than me. I could not really conceive of what would become of her if I took too much medication. On the other hand, I shuddered at the thought of her crashing with me in a vehicle that I purposely drove for that reason. Simultaneously, it was a hot day, and during the entire travel time, my dog was miserable, acted like she was overheating, and then seemed to hyperventilate.

In a split second, I turned my vehicle around and decided to return my dog to my house, leaving plenty of food and water for her as I had already done for my cats. I remember hoping that someone caring in my life, or even some other compassionate individual, would continue to take care of all my beloved pets in much the same manner as Mom and I had done. That thought allowed me to depart from my home once again even though it was extremely difficult. I traveled over an hour out of town but could still not determine the way to end my life. Before I knew it, I came back to my hometown and, of all things, ended up in the parking lot of a local store where I actually remained for hours on top of countless hours. I just sat there with all my thoughts still reverting to a plan. Every interrogative in the English language crossed my mind, including "Where, when, how" and "why." I knew my mother was gone forever, and I did not want to be in a world where she did not exist anymore. I began answering those questions in my mind.

I knew the "who," of course, was me in the middle of "what"— this bizarre situation. And "when" was right now. The "how" to end it all and to proceed concerned me the most. Left also were the questions of "where" to go and "why" all this had taken place at all. I felt so confused, so afraid, and in a state of complete hopelessness. I even wished that I had come to the realization of the event much sooner and had acted subsequently with my plan. The truth was that I had not been able to, but now I was going to. I did not sincerely believe that anything or anyone at all had the power to stop me. I felt as if I could not handle anything anymore, and for that matter, I did not want to. I have never felt that much worthlessness in my life. I had had many disappointments and many horrible occurrences in my past, but none of them could ever compare to this loss.

I had actually convinced myself a long time ago that this would be the scenario for me if Mom ever left me for good. I had not completely worked out the details. I believe the main reason for this failure too was never recognizing that an actual expectancy of death existed for that particular person in my life. There had already been two of the least-expected deaths in our family when my aunt and cousin both passed away at different intervals. Each one of these deaths completely shocked other family members, and they too were almost impossible with which to deal. Yet somehow, we had made it this far, but I personally will never ever forget those events. I do believe sincerely that the impacts of each of these were enormous upon my own life because my aunt was like a second mother to me, while my cousin, with whom I had closely grown up, was like a sister to me.

Now I was supposed to comprehend and accept this same result for my own mother. I simply could and would not. As I sat in that store parking lot, I could recall that my phone was constantly ringing and sounding off that numerous texts were being sent to me. I had ignored all calls up to this point, but something tugged at me to look at and answer these then. They were all from my youngest and eldest second cousins. Initially, fear and uncertainty would not allow me to speak to them. I could not face explaining anything about my mom—their great aunt. I could not detail my current and final plans to them either. I remember feeling like a sad little child who could not face those in her life who would demand answers concerning events that I could barely comprehend myself, much less face.

A certain amount of time passed, but when I received a text the next time, it was not from my cousins. Rather, it came from a neighbor who assumed that I was home at the time. I believe this occurred late in the afternoon or early in the evening. That text asked me if the ambulance, police cars, fire trucks, etc...at my house were for me. I, taken aback, was unsure what to respond, but I typed back, "No." She answered, "Good." Then, as I finished doing so, I literally felt the weight of the whole world crashing down upon me. Reality had set in, and I was expected now more than ever to accept it as well as go on with my plan of action.

My emotions were all over the place. I panicked; I feared everything. I cried uncontrollably as I realized that my mother was actually dead. I realized too that others must be aware of that fact also. Extreme horror and hopelessness surrounded my being. I could barely breathe and felt that I was experiencing another extreme anxiety attack. I froze. I felt all alone.

When my youngest second cousin—who had previously dialed me a huge number of times—rang me again, I answered. I only did so because I felt a strong need to answer that I cannot explain really well. It was actually one of the most unusual forms of persuasion that I had ever felt. It was as if my heart was being tugged to answer. When I finally did, I remember telling him that my life was over just as my mother's was. I said that I had no purpose anymore. I even told him that I had no reason to go on living since the one person on whom I could always count on—my precious mother—was gone. At some point in the conversation, he asked me over and over again where I was. I never answered.

When I began to cry, he cried with me, but mostly he tried to reason with me in a manner I never expected but will never forget either. I recall feeling as if I were communicating with a professional—a professional in the field of counseling—who diligently and wisely instructed me by telling me the best courses of action I could take regarding this severe situation. I had forgotten that he always did this regarding any topic that we ever discussed. Sometime also during the conversation, I understood that another relative had gone through a window at my house and discovered the body of my mother. Upon detecting this and whatever else I left there, especially the notes, he rightly contacted the proper authorities. That person later told me that he informed law officials too, because of the situation and his concern for my personal safety.

He obviously had read, I thought, each written message that I left at the house. He also said that officers merely told him to notify them if he heard from me. That was all. There was no mention of searching for me. The present and tender words of my youngest cousin, as stated above, impressed upon my mind intensely. He, in that phone conversation, among other things, advised me to come home right away and to deal with the situation. I repeated, over and over again, crying intensely, that I just could not do that. I reiterated that I no longer had the will to live, but something unexpected happened. His following words pierced my heart the most. Being a teenager and very much my junior, in comparison to my mature age, he explained that nothing—absolutely nothing—warranted my ending my own life.

At that time, I remembered that I had actually heard this statement on a television program that I viewed weeks ago. He furthermore stated that no matter the situation, my family would support and stand by me. His concern and love for me meant the world. His final comments, however, impacted me the most. At that time, he emotionally begged me not to end my life because, he said, my mom and I had been his "saving grace" when his own mother died unexpectedly at the age of fifty-three. It is very hard even now for me to describe what these words meant and mean to me. They truly gave me the will to try to live, live not only through this horrible situation, but also to actually try to live again. His heartfelt words gave me hope for the possible future. They also persuaded me to think about all the past times that my mother, he, and I shared right after his mother's untimely passing. We had even had many happy times prior to that, and we were so close to one another.

After her death, there were numerous occasions during which he spent the night at our house, and I recalled many Alabama Crimson Tide football games that we, as true fans, viewed together. In fact, my loving mother was the most genuine Bama fan ever. My mom's football influence on him had been immense. After his tender words, I even thought about all the serious talks all of us shared about so many subjects including, but not limited to, sports, current events, religion, and simple happenings during a school day or even stories of the past. We had laughed and cried together so many times too. His loving words—simple and complex as they were—saved me at that very moment! They—even expected and unexpected as they were—touched me in ways that only God and I could understand so deeply.

I, at some point later, figured out also that only God could have pushed me to answer my cousin's call. I also recognized that God had given him the strength and the courage to speak with me. I thought that besides me, only God could have known how long in my life I had waited to hear these words of appreciation from one of the children—my own second cousins—who were left when their mother died. At that time, I had tried my utmost to help them go on with life, despite this tragic loss.

My cousin's loving words were the beginning of the solution to the dilemmas that I now faced. They were my saving grace at the time that I needed them the most. They were, in essence, my lifeline to existence on earth. Honestly! They too are probably the most impressionable words that I have ever been touched by, and I will never forget them. That is how significant and needed they were then and are sometimes now when I struggle with life and its unexpected and discouraging circumstances. One fact was certain to me though. My youngest cousin knew God. In fact, we had discussed him and the topics of religion and spirituality numerous times. During these discussions too, he often, probably without his knowledge, made me feel ashamed when he seemed to know more on the subject than I felt I did. I, more importantly, admired this knowledge within him. In fact, it made me extremely proud. I was surer than ever of one thing though. God, as he often does on many occasions, placed my cousin right on the phone with me, right at that exact time, and with those right, or correct, words no doubt to aid me at this moment.

How miraculous is that? Extremely, because his recitations actually prevented me from carrying on with that final plan to end my life because the ugly and cruel aspects of life had pushed me to the lowest point ever. Amazing enough, our Lord and Savior strategically positioned my youngest cousin with me and entrusted him with the means of God's strength to initiate what I call my "deliverance" from the evil that tightly gripped me. The truth is that I might not be here today if this had never happened. That is a miracle for certain! I have to admit, however, that at one point, hearing this from him also made me somewhat angry—angry that he dared to mess up, not my best plans, but my plan to leave this world. I know this message from him was God—sent because God knew that of all the people in my life, this cousin was the one who could have influenced me the most in this particular situation.

After this conversation with my relative, other events followed. I slept very little that evening. My cousin checked on me several times by phone to see if I was okay. I also promised my family members that I would plan to speak with the local authorities regarding the situation no later than tomorrow morning. I really did not know how I was going to deal with any of this. I made myself physically sick just thinking about all this.

# CHAPTER SIX

# The Unexpected Embarrassment of a Lifetime

*The Lord seeth not as man seeth; for man looketh on the*
*outward appearance, but God looketh on the heart.*

—1 Samuel 16: 7

February 12 was the next morning. I frantically attempted to contact local law officers with the intent of setting up a time to answer their questions concerning the previous events. Secondary to this was my concern regarding the whereabouts of my pets left at my home. I wondered if any of them had been removed from the house that former evening and if they had been taken to an animal shelter. My phone calls regarding both subjects—Mom and my pets—seemed useless as I received, numerous times, answering machine messages rather than speaking to actual persons themselves. In my countless attempts to connect, I finally spoke to one gentleman only, explained my situation, and during the conversation felt even more frustration when my questions failed once again to be answered.

The guy was "unable to help me" and "did not know what to tell me" because "no one was present in any of the offices contacted." He claimed that he had no valuable information himself to pass on to me. Then he merely suggested that I leave messages again and wait for return phone calls. I cannot describe how frustrating this was then. My panic and uncertainty increased 100 percent. I began to react on the issues of my pets. I, still highly frustrated, decided to have my eldest cousin take me to my house—the place to which I previously planned no return. I wanted to see if my pets were where I left them. It also occurred to me that my home was left unlocked after the past days' events. He acquiesced, and upon our arrival, I immediately searched for the possibility of yellow crime tape encircling the house. I did not think of this because I thought I had committed a crime. Rather, it just came to mind because of the descriptions I had received regarding the situation.

My cousins assured me, though, that the police did not make a big deal out of wanting to speak to me then. They also indicated to me that no hint of a crime even came up in conversations that night. There was no such yellow tape. That fact made me feel more secure about my entry. I still did not really want to physically be there—the location of so much unhappiness and despair in my life now. As I was about to enter, I felt as if there was somewhat of a "dryness" or emptiness upon the house that my mother and I now formerly inhabited together. I was sad and dejected to go in the place where she no longer was, and I simply dreaded doing so. Fear and apprehensiveness pierced me too, yet I, almost ill once again, entered the door—unlocked as I suspected—alone as my relative, who had to be experiencing some uncertainty and fear himself, waited in his car at the bottom of my driveway close to the street.

When I walked in, the stench was as horrible as it had been the day I left. A handful or more of blankets were strewn all over the living room floor. Her recliner was still there, but the sight of it made me sick. Items had been moved and shuffled all over the place. I could hardly contain myself. I cried aloud and actually thought that I would never be able to stop. I couldn't wait to get out of there. Suddenly, the real reason why I was there came back to me—my pets. I found all my cats present, but my precious and beloved dog was nowhere to be found. My heart sank again, and I cried the entire time that I went through every single room of the house, calling her by name. I even thought she might surface from some hiding place that she sought during the previous night's chaotic occurrences. I was able to consider this because my eldest cousin had been told, by local authorities, that my dog would not be removed from the house that night but, perhaps, the next day.

It was obvious to me, however, that she had already been taken away—destination unknown—and I was crushed. I cried and cried. I returned to my cousin and begged him to find out where she was and to please get her back for me. As much as I wanted this accomplished too, I just could not emotionally and even physically handle the task myself right now. He agreed to do the best he could. I hope one day he knows how much better this made me feel at that terrible time. We returned to my female cousin's house. Because of all the situations at hand, I felt uneasy, uncomfortable, sad, and even out of place around my own family members. I did not know how to act, what to say, etc., and they were just as confused and unsure as I was. They did not know how to act either. I understood all this also because of all the crazy details of the whole—what I considered a horrible mess—situation. I recall that very little conversation took place. I felt a strong need to exit the premises immediately.

In my mind, the whole subject matter and events following were too raw to even consider a meaningful discussion among all present. I sincerely remember being emotionally upset and wanting more compassion than I received from anyone. I could only imagine their thoughts concerning me, but I absorbed a great deal of negativity.

I decided that the best thing for me to do was leave, and I did just that. I do remember saying to them that I would desperately wait on a return call from the police. I was not patient, so I attempted to call them, again to no avail. As I departed, my eldest cousin promised once again to retrieve my beloved dog if possible. Although many of my thoughts were clouded at this time, I also willingly accepted his offer to take care of my dog, if found, at his house if needed. I believe God orchestrated this offer for me since I could not return to my house to stay right now. I still did not know where I was going stay myself. I secretly wished for one of my family members to offer this, but it never happened.

I was grateful that my dog had a place, though, because this was one less worry for me to have. I had no solution for myself, but later on God blessed me with a true friend who graciously allowed me to remain at her home. Still outside my cousin's place, I decided to, in the meantime, go to a store to buy dog food and new locks for my still-unprotected house doors. I had a sense of hope of my dog being retrieved. That was why I wanted to get the pet food in the first place. During all these moments, I surprised myself by being able to handle such tasks after the realization of my mother's death. My trip to the store was brief, and afterward I returned to my female cousin's home to give the other relative the purchased dog food.

I need to say also that I was totally unaware of the events to follow. When I arrived, no one was home. I remained in my vehicle. My eldest cousin came, and upon my invitation, he and I sat there in my van talking over the recent events. I, at one point, detected that he acted a little peculiar, but I could not figure what the difference in his manner was. I also remember that it was raining extremely hard, and suddenly I noticed, in the rearview mirror, three vehicles pull up behind my van. Without actually knowing the truth, I felt a sudden sensation that they were arriving for me. I then realized that one vehicle was a police car, one was a van of some sort, and the other was a car with an unusual antenna.

I looked at my cousin and said, "You knew this was going to happen." I was so angry but knew I had to comply. Later on, I discovered that he was just obeying the police when they said to let them know if he heard from me. I do not have the words to write here how stunned I was at this moment. I honestly never expected this scene once in my mind. I have stated before that I was unaware of any crime. I just expected a return call from officers after all the messages I had desperately left. Initially, as my cousin and I exited my van, I heard one official question me as to who got out of the vehicle with me. Upon hearing this, I felt that this questioning seemed to almost suggest that I and my "conspirator" had just stepped outside the vehicle. I believe that the officer's strong and bold tone in asking made me feel this way.

I think both of us—my cousin included—answered that question simultaneously. I felt that my cousin eagerly identified himself as the one who had talked to him previously. I recall that the detective, whom I recognized immediately, motioned for me to move closer. I can see and feel the coldness of the rapidly falling rain on me even now. I remember moving slowly toward him. I also recall the fear that gripped my entire body as all my tears began to flow down my face. Astonished as I was, I managed at one point to tell all present that I had tried to call numerous times this morning, left messages, and received no return calls. I added that I wanted to arrange a time to be interrogated regarding my mother. Not one person present said a word. I truly hated being ignored because I considered what I had to say significant. My statements did not seem to matter, but I did agree to go for questioning—what I had attempted to arrange by phone all morning.

Never having been a part of anything like this, I innocently asked if I was to follow them to police headquarters in my van. Then one of the detectives said, "Actually, we are going to do it this way." Shockingly enough to me, the female police officer walked up and handcuffed me. I found this so unbelievable. I do not think I said anything. I do not remember any rights being read to me. Had this occurred, I would definitely have remembered it. Before I was told to get into the back of the police car, the officer asked me if I, as she put it, "had any weapons or anything with which to stick her." My response, of course, was an adamant, "No!" I almost wanted to laugh aloud at the thought of her questioning, but I did not. I really could not believe that I, who had always tried to do the right thing, was even being asked this. It seemed so strange and far-fetched for me to be hearing her words. I thought over and over how I honestly never expected any of this. I dejectedly assumed that I was being arrested. I cannot explain what a shock this was to me.

All three vehicles then proceeded to the downtown precinct. It was a ride, I promise you, that I had never experienced before in my life. I complied as I cried incessantly. I kept thinking that I had lived all my life in this town and had never traveled in this manner to the local police station. I guarantee that I was totally embarrassed, unprepared for such a trip, and absolutely scared to death. To say I was mortified was a true understatement. I experienced the worst feelings that I had ever had. I was somewhat physically ill and still in tears the whole way. Even though I was familiar with the surroundings of all the city offices, I somehow lost all sense of knowledge of any of these places as I rode, still handcuffed, with my hands behind my back. The tightness of these hurt tremendously. I could hardly move, but there was nothing I could do about any of this—absolutely nothing. I just wanted it to end.

Still unfamiliar with my so-called familiar surroundings, I can honestly state that when I got out of the squad car, I could not really identify with anything. I could only follow instructions. I remember going up several outdoor steps. I was wearing a knee brace on my left leg because of a torn meniscus. Climbing steps was difficult anyway. I remember commenting aloud about how hard it was for me to walk with the brace, much less with the unexpected cuffs around my wrists. I was in pain. Yet I continued. No experience had ever affected me in this manner. My emotions were all over the place, but I could only, once again, comply—comply with what? I had no idea what was ahead. I was scared to find out, but I had no choice in the matter.

# CHAPTER SEVEN

# The Legal System

Our law does not judge a man unless it first hears
from him and knows what he is doing, does it?
—John 4:51

My experiences with the legal system of our city were numerous and so new to me. With the knee brace and cuffs, I did physically make it up the hateful stairs. I do remember feeling as if I would fall several times because of the weakness of my knee and because of the deterioration of my spirit. Then I was led to a rather bleak interrogation room with a table and some chairs. Prior to questioning, the handcuffs were removed. I was also asked to empty my coat pockets. I recall that I had brought my driver's license in a little purse, having initially believed that I was to drive to the station myself. I also was carrying two bottles of medication with me, incidentally the two I held for my final plan to cease my existence on earth. All this was removed from my possession during questions but immediately given back to me afterward.

I thought that, at that time, it was strange for the medication to be returned after my written notes regarding possible suicide were left at my house. I put them all back in my jacket pocket anyway. Before the return of them, however, present then in the interrogation room were two detectives and I. They had papers of some sort in front of them. I had already cried during the entire ride there, and I continued sobbing during the rest of the process. I just could not control my sadness. I was still terrified to be there. I remember feeling as if my body were totally gripped in fear. First, I was asked if I wished to have a lawyer present. I had no idea how to answer that question. I, never having been in trouble before, declined. I remember thinking too that I had done nothing wrong to my knowledge. If I had known then what I know now regarding the events, I would have requested an attorney in a heartbeat. If I had done so, I could have saved myself a great deal of grief. What this means is I would have had a witness, and the discrepancies that I detected later, perhaps, could have been avoided. I will discuss this soon in a chapter.

As the questioning began, the lead detective made the statement to me that he assumed fear had played a major role in the entire event. I nodded, thinking that I was so scared to face even the thought of my mother dying. Later, I wondered in my mind what he actually interpreted this to mean. When I was asked why I did not call 911, I could only say that I must have panicked at the thought of my mother dying. This was something I never wanted to encounter, much less accept ever. The detective then asked me if I put all the blankets on top of my mother at once. I found this question odd but answered no. His next interrogation was about the air fresheners that I purchased. He wanted to know if I got them all at the same place and all at once. Since I recalled buying them at different stores at different times, that was my response. His only comment was that I had spent a fortune on these. I simply nodded. The question then regarded the time that I remained at my home. The detective wanted to know the exact day I left the premises for good. I remember a distinct look of surprise—maybe even shock—upon his face when I responded. The truth was that I had remained there every night—overnight—until the evening of February 11, the day of the discovery of her body.

He then asked how I knew of the police's presence at my home on this specific date. I explained that a neighbor texted me about all the emergency vehicles there that day. I added too that I had spoken by phone with two of my cousins who had been present at the house also. After all these questions, I, still vividly upset and in tears, remember thinking to myself that this was quite a varied array of questions. I also thought that I sincerely answered each one, but in my mind, these did not cover the entire series of events. I, not used to any of these procedures, said nothing about any of that, however. I am sure that my silence was also influenced by my fear of being here in the first place and my strong desire to get out of there as soon as possible. Do I regret this lack of speech now? You better believe I certainly do. Thinking of this matter also makes me regret not having an attorney present on my behalf either. My analysis of this whole legal process now is much clearer currently than it was then. What this means is that I was unable at that actual moment to assess where this whole situation was actually headed. In other words, I was not prepared for the actuality of it all.

At the time that I needed to be grieving for what I now knew was the loss of my mother, I was in a police station, after apparently being arrested for the first time in my life, answering questions without even being aware of what I was being accused. During the questioning, at one point the lead detective asked me the significance of four thirty in the morning. I knew he must be referring to the note I left at my house the last day I was there. I had written that Mom died peacefully at that time of morning. I said the date was December 29 also. I explained that, before leaving that day, I realized that Mom took her last breath the day after my female cousin had her second child. I also said that I looked at my mantel clock just as Mom cried out that morning. I do not recall any response to my words. I also added that my little cousin was staying with us at that time. I said that he was present during everything. My comment prompted another question by the second officer in the room. I noticed that he had been silent prior to this moment. He began by claiming that he had seen a homemade picture that day at my house with a February 2019 date written on it.

Right then, I could visualize that picture. It was one of a group of valentine stickers, items that I had purchased myself. I bought those red-and-pink stickers for my little cousin to make a holiday picture. He loved these and creating things. I explained that with the help of his mother, he had made this picture for me at his own house. Then, one day, when I gave them a ride—from their home—I told him that he came running out of his house excitedly and gave it to me. I could actually remember the broad smile on his little face that morning. I even told the detective that receiving this gift was a treasure of a lifetime to me. I also wanted to tell him how much stuff like this meant to me, but I decided not to do so. His question regarding this piece of art was if the little boy had created it at my home while my mother's body was there.

I told him, "Of course not," but I could certainly understand his confusion because of the date written on it. I furthermore stated that I used to be a teacher, dating all the artwork, crafts, etc. of my former students. I also said that I had placed the February date—the day that he actually gave it to me—to cherish the time he thought of me as well as to have the knowledge that, as a preschooler, he had completed this form of art just for me. His response? "Cool." Although this was a short and unexpected answer to me, I was stunned. I was not so taken aback by his answer, but by my own thoughts then. I now realized that this whole situation was a real deal, which I was going to face even though I never intended to harm anyone. I also did not know I had broken a law. Every piece of it—the event—floored me. I also knew that I could do nothing about any of it but comply.

I finally was able to ask the detective if I was going to jail. I feared the answer to this question more than anything. He answered: "Jail is for criminals, Joni. You are not a criminal." At this point, I could not help but feel a tiny bit of relief. He also stated that my mother must have died of natural causes—"Probably a heart attack." He then declared that he knew that I loved my mother, and he also claimed that he knew how close we were. This made me feel even more relieved though I was still upset. You see, Mom and I knew this detective. We had actually visited his mother once with another friend to invite her to the church we were attending. It is interesting to note too that at the time of this visit, the very detective questioning me was an infant whom I held in my arms that very day. I was younger then but cannot remember my age at the time. During the whole period of interrogation, I could not get the memory of this visit out of my mind. I remember that I kept thinking, *What a small world!* Having asked about jail, I waited anxiously hoping for good news.

At that moment, he stood up and walked over to me. I wondered what was happening next. He began telling me that as upset as I was, I needed to understand that in telling no one of the situation, I apparently broke the law. He told me the code number, but I had no clue as to what he said. I was too flabbergasted by his initial revelation as he walked toward me. At some point, he may have used the word *felony* in the conversation. I honestly cannot remember. At some moment, he told me that one of three things would happen to me. He said I could go to jail, I could be placed in a holding cell with a bond, or I could be released on my own recognizance—allowing me to return to wherever I was staying. I would have a court date also. I prayed hard on the spot for the last option.

He also told me that I, if released, must of course show up for my intended court date. At the time, I kept thinking that if the detective wanted to scare me, he certainly had done so. I feared all of what faced me. I could never see myself in a jail cell. I could never handle that for sure. This thought made me fear the outcome. This was also coupled with the whole shock of everything, including Mom's death and this entire police station visit. I never knew that such a law, which I apparently broke, existed. In other words, I never intentionally broke the law. The legalities, jail time, or whatever never entered my mind until I stood right in that interrogation room. All this was because I could not accept my own mother's death. That was the crux of this whole scenario. I was not going to lose her because she was everything to me. I simply—even though it was not simple in the least—could not let her go.

I emphasize too that I never grieved the entire time prior to February 11, 2019. I am certain that grief never hit me until then. I, to a degree, accepted her death since reality fully set in when denial left. I must say "to a degree" because all this legal mess, discussions, and eventually court itself prevented me really from being able to fully grieve. When the sorrow began, I had never felt the feelings that I experienced then and now. I knew too that the words that my mother often said were so true. She declared, "You only have one mother." I always realized that these words rang true, but for me to have to live with that idea, along with her passing, was another matter. I never wanted my one mother in the world to be gone. I never wanted to hear or know that I would never see her on earth again. I thought about how incomparable to any of my other relationships the one with her was. I realized also that I had experienced death before Mom's, and it was totally despairing. Yet it seemed impossible at any time to experience Mom's passing. The mixture of feelings it has caused are those which I would never wish upon another person ever. This journey has caused me to fear, to be sad, and to be terribly unsure of anything. It has made me recognize that how close we were in relationship has allowed these horrible feelings to prevail. My thoughts, as the detective ushered me to my fate? They were *How could the closest person ever to me—far closer than anyone else—go away?*

After hearing the explanation of my three options for release that day—or not—I recall that, at first, I did not really know what a magistrate was. I asked the officer, but I was so upset, confused, and overwhelmed that I did not remember what he said. I just followed instructions, still feeling that the whole picture was too far-fetched to grasp its reality. I only knew that every bit of it was taking place. I, like a programmed robot, did exactly what I was told. I did not know what else to do. None of my experiences had been like this one.

Prior to the meeting with the magistrate, I was handcuffed again, and at some point, my ankles were cuffed also. I felt this action was because of the felony charge itself. I cannot really describe how uncomfortable these were. They felt as bad as the first ones when I came in the building. I have already mentioned my messed-up knee. Well, the addition of the ankle shackles just added to my pain. I did mention this to the officer, but his answer was that this was how most people view being confined. My uneasiness pervaded. I also almost fell once or twice because I actually forgot that they were on, especially when I sat down and got back up again. Hurting, I could only think that I had never done anything like this. I believed it was all crazy—total insanity. Shortly the detective and I, shackled by both cuffs, went into a room where there was a magistrate sitting down. I did not remember much said at that time but was pretty sure that an explanation of the charge against me was the focal point. One thing I do recall, however, was this question—from the magistrate himself—directed to me: "Do you have anything to say?"

I, a little calmer but still crying, declared: "I loved my mother more than anything." Not expecting this response, the detective, not the magistrate, stated: "Amen! I know how close you and your mother were." I did not really know what to say. Before the magistrate's final decision, this same detective whispered to me that I would be released after signing a paper to report back to court on a specific day. I remember muttering, "Thank God!" aloud. Little did I celebrate though. I felt a little serenity and a little relief but had no idea what else was in store for me. I just wanted to get out of there. The whole place stifled me, and I could hardly breathe. It was, unfortunately, not over for me yet. More extremely upsetting surprises and practices awaited me. It seemed to me to be a total crash course in the legal system about which I knew little and which I never expected. I know too that it was an experience of which I needed to be free but wasn't.

Following the magistrate, the detective told me to go to another area where other procedures would take place. He actually told me to just go and sit down in another area. I believe it was the sheriff's department because everyone was dressed in those brown uniforms, which were the uniforms of the officers of that department. Before I actually went, however, the officer informed me that when I went in there, there would be two guys in handcuffs standing at the desk. He actually told me not to pay any attention to these guys and to merely sit down. I was a bit puzzled but nodded. I did see the two handcuffed men. To my knowledge, they never turned around and looked at me. I only viewed them and their actions from behind. A good deal of the sheriff deputies, all dressed in brown, however, stared at me. This really bothered me and made me feel extremely uncomfortable. I wished right then that they had something better to do then to look at me.

In my opinion, the whole experience was hard enough to endure, let alone this. Regarding the two handcuffed men, I recall a bit of joking between them and the detective who instructed me to this area. This definitely made me feel that they had previously met, probably in this same place. Another portion of my time was spent being fingerprinted. The detective who directed me to this area performed this activity after speaking with the local sheriff. I was embarrassed when the latter, whom I already knew, said, "Hello, Miss Joni." He then added, "I do not know what brings you here today. It is actually none of my business, but I do wish you the best." He was actually the DARE officer of my preschool class at one time at a local private school. Just imagine how uncomfortable for me it was to run into him during this mess. I really appreciated his friend-liness, but I just really wanted to run away. I was totally stunned, somewhat grateful, but could not release from my mind the thought that at another place, I once taught his son.

After the fingerprinting, I was asked to give a DNA swab to assist in identifying my mother's body, which had been sent to the medical examiner's office in Roanoke, Virginia, for an autopsy. I asked the detective if he recognized my mother. He said yes, but those in Roanoke, he claimed, wouldn't necessarily. His reason for this swab was that those living there were not familiar with her. I just did what I was told.

At some point too I had to be photographed. I remember that this process seemed to last indefinitely. I kept feeling that I was stand-ing, posing, for such a long time. I felt sick and wanted it to be over quicker than it ever was. It was in this area too that I heard the detective tell the female sheriff deputy, who filled out forms with me there, that it was "unsecured bond." I did not know really what that all entailed, but I could guess. No one explained it to me. Then, thank God, I was released! Prior to leaving, I want to say that this same female deputy casually said when I first came before her, "What brings you here today?" I have no idea how I answered that question, but I remember saying something.

Now and then, I still cannot believe that I experienced this entire situation. The one positive thing that I looked forward to was to hear that my loving dog had been retrieved—retrieved right before she was headed to the Scott County Virginia animal shelter. You see,

Bristol, Virginia's animal shelter was not complete then. I cannot believe that my dog was saved before going farther in the state of Virginia. Yet I was thrilled that she had been found in the first place. When I left the sheriff's department, I did think of some personal things. These were actually my opinions concerning the police station experience. Even though I had been so scared and so visually upset, I had one consolation. I did appreciate the manner in which the lead detective explained to me—step by step—the procedures through which I would be taken. I sincerely felt that he, at that time, realized how tormenting all this was for me and even how unfamiliar the entire law-breaking environment was to me. I actually felt, as they say, like a fish out of water. On top of that, my mother, whom I loved so deeply, was gone—gone forever. I did, in fact, appreciate his gestures enormously. This was one of the hardest tasks that I have ever had to perform. His regular comments were greatly appreciated by me at this time.

When I arrived back at my van—after my cousins brought me there—I was so drained, so depleted of energy. I had never experienced anything close to any of this, and it exhausted me to the fullest extent. That exhaustion, however, did not prevent me from constantly worrying about everything and from also being in total despair over my mother's death. More than anything, I wanted to disappear from the face of the earth—to go somewhere that released me from all this. Pain was what I completely felt all over my entire being. I had never had that type of pain either.

For the next month or so, my life was a whirlwind of uncertainty. I had no idea where I was going to stay at this time. Many other questions surfaced through my mind, such as "Where would I live now?" and "How would I continue on without my precious mother?" I even wondered, "How would I make it through this?" Those were hard questions for which I had no answers. I never thought I would find any either. In a short while, I decided to stay at a neighbor's, and her offer to help me was more than appreciated. My dog took up residence with my cousins as promised. This was temporary, of course. I am certain this was the most difficult time in my life. I was in complete limbo.

Regarding the legal system once again, I did not appear at the courthouse until a little over a month later, on March 19, 2019. This was my arraignment hearing, which was the time during which I formally faced charges regarding this whole mess. I remember being told that formal charge itself was a felony of concealing a body. I could hardly believe any of this. I could only do what I was told to do—appear. Upon entrance to the courthouse, to say that I was embarrassed by this situation was an understatement. I was extremely intimidated to see many local lawyers whose children I had taught as well as kept while they were out of town. After appearing before the judge, I was appointed a lawyer, and afterward I left so briskly because, truthfully, I could not wait to get out of there.

I was given a female attorney's name to contact. I began to think at this time about the characteristics that I wished my attorney to have while handling this case. I had never been in trouble, until now, so it was hard to imagine that I actually had to do this. Yet I did, God help me. I thought for a lengthy time and realized that I, of course, desired to have an attorney who would work to help me. I also felt that I wanted that individual to be hardcore but compassionate. I felt that with these traits, that person would truly care about me in this situation but also would perform in an excellent, professional, and extremely dedicated manner. I even wished for someone who would "tell it like it is," but still listen to what I had to say—my ideas, my opinions, and all my explanations of the situation at hand.

Another characteristic that a good friend pointed out to me was also considered—protection from the media as much as possible and from any other harmful forces that might attempt to tear me down without knowing all the facts and explorations regarding my case and my situation. In the best scenario ever, I thought too that I would wish that my legal representative would ideally believe me. I would watch carefully for demonstrations of this also. Similarly, I thought about how important it would be to me for that legal representative to believe that I was innocent. If that were not the case, I would still want that attorney's promise to defend me 100 percent, perhaps 110 percent, and to represent me in the best way possible.

Fortunately, and written a little prematurely in this book, I had an appointed lawyer who fulfilled all my expectations and more. I thank God so much for her guidance too. In addition, I recognized that her staff and personnel in her office seemed strongly dedicated to their jobs also. Each one of them made me feel served totally well because each one of them was courteous, compassionate, and caring. Every one too treated me with a good deal of respect when I encountered them or spoke to them by phone. At the end of my entire case, I was thrilled when the lawyer assured me that after the court decision, she would assist me with any questions that I had, especially concerning probation issues. I was so grateful for this. I said thank you and I gave her a hug. I told her how much I appreciated the security, respect, and admiration that she enabled me to feel with my case in her hands. She smiled and said that I was special. I believe that her appointment was an answer to prayer and one of the best blessings that I had but never expected.

My third encounter with the legal system came when I had to go to court in June of 2019. Prior to this date, one postponement for me existed in April of that same year. The June appearance was my preliminary hearing. I dreaded it more than anything. I kept thinking over and over again that all this was happening because I could not let her go. In my opinion, this was the perfect explanation for the entire situation. I reiterated in my thoughts that I knew nothing about a law that I broke. My mind was set on one notion: "I cannot bear to lose my beautiful mother. This is not fair. I hate this cruel and hateful world." I also wanted to depart from it right then.

On this particular day, two of my true friends accompanied me to court, and I will forever be thankful for their presence, their love, and their undying support. They proudly walked in by my side— gently talking about how all was going to be okay. I was not so sure about that, but I had no choice but to attend the horrific event. I did, however, feel if they had not been with me, I would have reacted very differently. I imagine I would have had some sort of breakdown. I kept thinking over and over again in my mind, *God help me.* Someone once told me if you cannot explain all your troubles to him, and you need comfort, "Help me" will do. I had tested this theory before and hoped it worked just as well during what was probably a worse time than the other one was. I do, however, appreciate the hugs, the smiles, and the unending support of my two staunch friends. This, among many other things, demonstrated to me their genuine friendship and love for me. I also knew that I had their respect. No one can ever believe how thankful I was for that.

I did not really know what was going to happen. I had several possible scenarios running through my mind, and each of these made me sick to my stomach. Initially, I believed that I might go to jail. There, I knew I would never make it. I remember telling my pastor and his wife those thoughts days earlier. They, the best Christians ever, matter-of-factly said, "God knows that already." They had given me comfort because I had forgotten that throughout this entire ugly and tragic ordeal. I had prayer with another one of our ministers the night before court too. I remember crying profusely as I honestly said then, "I am scared—really, really scared." I hope that he realizes one day that in response to the numerous things I said, he often repeated, "Sure you are. Sure you are." This gave me relief too. He made me believe that he was really concerned for me. I also felt that he knew how hard all this was for me. I truly thought I would never make it literally to this point.

Before entering the building—the courthouse—a great deal of fear gripped my being. I feared media circus frenzy would take place. In fact, I could envision the sensationalism already! I too was afraid of untruths and nonfacts, especially printed by those reporters. Fortunately, at this time, I was not the least bit aware of any of this taking place. I was more than thrilled with this assumption.

Unlike the preliminary hearing, on this crucial court date, I was ecstatic when my appointed attorney directed us to sit on one of the benches outside rather than inside the courtroom. The latter had always affected me negatively. Being able to remain here allowed calmness to surround me. I know that the fear would never quite leave me, but because of the seating arrangement a good deal of the panic did. I hoped too that this would enable me to handle matters better.

While seated outside the courtroom, I heard these words from my lawyer: "I am going right now to meet with the commonwealth's attorney. I may have a bit of good news." She also stated that she had spoken on the phone to him this week. I honestly did not know whether to be optimistic or not. I just sat quietly as she departed and tried not to worry. The following waiting time, however, seemed to endure forever. When she returned, she requested my presence in a private room near the courtroom itself.

My heart throbbed as I entered the room. My thoughts were *What is going to happen to me?* and *Can I handle this?* Then the explanation by her of the offer began. Apparently, I was being offered a deal to plead guilty to a lower-class misdemeanor rather than to a low-class felony. My attorney further stated that I would be pleading to an "improper disposal of a body" charge. Yet we both agreed that I never disposed of the body. Secondly, she claimed that the felony charge was still concealing a body. In accepting the first charge, I would receive supervised probation for a year. I later realized too that this included a suspended twelve-month jail sentence suspended by the judge himself. Otherwise, she informed me that I would face the felony, and if pleading innocent, I would go to trial and have no guarantee of an innocent verdict. My attorney further explained that if I agreed to the misdemeanor, I could plead no contest, rather than straight-out guilty.

I was totally blown away by all this. I honestly did not know what to do. I am sure that my attorney could read both these reactions upon my sullen face. I was puzzled. I have never been the type of individual who could make snap decisions, especially one like this with so much riding on it. I was uncomfortable with any type of "guilty" plea because I know that I did what I did because I could not face my own mother's death. I never considered anything else at the time, such as law-breaking or any of this for that matter. I kept reminding myself of this and my inability to accept Mom's permanent absence from this earth. It hurt more than anything to realize that Mom would be away from me for the rest of my life here. Saying I was guilty of disposing of her body just sounded sick to me. I had never done any such thing, and I was having a real tough time handling how it all came to this. I looked confusingly at my lawyer, but I knew that she could not tell me what to do. I also did not have much time to think about all this. I then thought to myself that pleading to a lower charge with lower consequences was logically better than the reverse. I was never comfortable with the concealing charge either because despite how it looked to everyone, I never intended to do this, much less break the law in doing so. I was confused, in shock, and above all in a place then in which I was unable to react. Her death had paralyzed me tremendously.

At this time, I thought too that anyone who really knew me, knew this, and understood it, at least to a certain point. As I was ruminating, my lawyer informed me that if I felt more comfortable saying that no contest, with a guilty plea, that was possible. She said that those uncomfortable speaking aloud in an open courtroom often utilized no contest. It was, however, the next piece of info that almost made me lose my mind. She said in her meeting, that if I did not accept the misdemeanor, the police would go forth with not only a felony, but they would pursue "malicious intent" against my own mother. I was honestly floored—literally shocked beyond belief. My lawyer recognized this, and she was quick to agree with me that there never was such intent, and I so appreciated the recognition of the truth. The whole intent aspect to these cases more than angered and infuriated me because I never did anything in this situation to intentionally harm my mother.

Outraged as I was, it could only last temporarily since I was forced back to the reality of the court situation now. After my thoughts drifted for a little bit more, I looked at the one who had defended me to the utmost, protected me, and had compassionately dealt with this entire situation, just as it should have been. With tears in my eyes, I said, "As much as I know my innocence in this mixed-up mess, I just want this to be over!" She nodded. She knew very well how much I loved my mother. She further recognized that none of this process had ever been easy for me, not one single bit. If I summed it up myself, I would declare that I went through pure hell and was still left to deal with the unexpected passing of my dear mother—an even greater hell with which to deal. I had cried out to me so many times: "How can any of this be? How can I even begin to handle any of it?" I also felt, on more than one occasion, like giving up completely.

My attorney calmed my nerves when she began telling me a story about a close friend of hers and that friend's mother. She spoke about the loss that her friend experienced with her close parent. I knew she was trying to make me feel better. I really appreciated that. When it was decided that I would enter a plea of guilty to the lower charge, I made sure to tell her that I desired to plea the no contest. I felt better with this, but there was not really much comfort where any of this was concerned.

It was then time to enter that dreaded courtroom. Fortunately, I once again got to sit outside it—this time until the bailiff notified me. I knew that my lawyer probably orchestrated this, and I appreciated it immensely. That fact honestly helped me to make it a little more. When called to the courtroom, no one knew this but me and God. I was so unfamiliar with the way things operated; I walked in and nervously looked for my lawyer. I almost panicked for a second or two simply because all eyes were on me—all the eyes of the courtroom audience, attorneys, judge, and whoever was there. I had failed to hear the bailiff say, "Go stand in front of the judge."

Once again, my practical sense was at the back door. When I did spot her, I hurriedly took my proper place. My attorney, the commonwealth's attorney, and I—all three—stood in front of a judge. This was where final papers were to be signed. The judge did not ask me, as I expected, "How do you plea?" He looked at the commonwealth's attorney and said, "So that's guilty?" He nodded and softly said yes. As I managed to look over at him, I could not help but see what I thought was an extreme look of concern—perhaps total confusion—upon his countenance. Part of me could understand this. In fact, I never wanted to look at him because my family and I had known him for years. In fact, Mom and I had attended church with him and his family.

The judge then looked at me and said, "So do you agree, Ms. Overlook?"

I merely answered either "Yes, sir, I do," or "Yes, your honor, I do." I cannot remember which was used. It ended at that and with all our signatures. But not really. I was relieved, but it was a different kind of relief from the normal one. What I mean is that I felt a little freedom at this time but mostly dread—dread to deal with a life without my mom. I was upset too that I had not been able to plead no contest, as formerly discussed. I told myself that no matter if I said guilty or no contest, both of these meant guilty. I had just wanted to save face a bit by not uttering that latter word, which, to me, denoted a terrible connotation. This whole matter had been so traumatic on many levels. Then, after expressing gratitude to my lawyer, hugs with those great friends who stood by my side, the three of us rode the elevator to the first floor and finally exited out of the courthouse door. All of us were relieved, but it was so emotional too. I know there were some tears also. One of my friends asked me if I were going to Sonic to get cherry limeade. I had to laugh because I had told her before that I needed this desperately. Before we parted, I hugged both of them and told them that they would never know how much their love and support had meant to me. I could not have been more sincere about anything.

When I got into my vehicle, my relief became a little short-lived. I thought about having to meet court requirements, something I had never had to do. I considered that I had never been on probation, much less supervised probation, in my life. I told myself that I did not know what to expect. I finally reconciled myself to a calming point, which has never been easy for me. I thought about how I could only to the best of my ability to comply with all this. "I have no choice anyway," I repeated to myself. Then, I, in my van, sat and thanked God intensely for what he had just done for me. It was a true miracle, in my opinion, a definite true miracle. Deep down, I knew too that I must face the further circumstances associated with this whole scenario. Yet I praised God because through him I had made it this far. I still had trouble believing that I was actually alive right now. Before pulling out of the courthouse lot, I thanked God, was unaware of any media personnel on this day. Yet as I would soon learn, their reporting still existed.

The remaining hours of my day were spent calling and notifying close friends and family about the entire morning. My pastor's wife, who had been to court with me, was actually on the phone with the preacher himself when I tried to call him. The most touching of events took place with this conversation. I will never ever forget that he informed me that he knew what had happened. Then he cried. He cried because all the emotions, all the stress, and all the tensions of this entire court and legal event had just ended. He was, I suspect, in awe of our awesome God and all that he had done. His reaction touched me immensely because we had prayed about, discussed, and gone over the entire events so many times before this day. To me, it seemed like a lifetime—a lifetime of ups and downs, spinning around in so many circles of circumstances that a feeling of relief had to be had now.

The pastor confirmed for me how he cared about me and the outcome. I was deeply touched. I was thankful for discussions with his wife, my good friend, too. I was happy that throughout all this, God had given me another friend and counselor who also went to bat for me by meeting with my lawyer prior to the current day's events. I was deeply affected by the presence of my other friend in court who had come to be with me without hesitation. Would you believe that I babysat her two girls when they were little and that I even had her grandchildren in the church day care where I worked? I was happy to speak with all my genuine friends and family who stood by me throughout this process. "It was a good day after all," I said to myself. Yet I knew it was going to be more than difficult to realize the passing of my mom.

# CHAPTER EIGHT

# Judgment, Privacy, and the Media

Give thanks in all circumstances; for this is
God's will for you in Jesus Christ.
—1 Thessalonians 5:18

I have often wondered if I failed in this situation. I believe that I did, especially when viewed by society's standards. I know that there were individuals who judged matters in my case from the so-called outside without knowing all the true details on the inside. I believe this happens all the time. I know too that many friends, strangers, and some of my own family members did exactly this. From a personal standpoint, I strongly think that many of us want to always do the right thing in every single event that occurs in our lives. I recognize on the other hand, that this is an ideal—unattainable— goal that no one can achieve simply because each one is human. I realize also that only God, the almighty and powerful one, is able to do this—the impossible. I am certain of that. I think too that some individuals can achieve what seems impossible but only with God's strength in their lives.

I reflect too upon other aspects of this case, and I wonder if the system failed me regarding my mother's death. I believe the answer to that question is twofold. In some ways it did, while in other ways it helped me. I know that is such a contradiction, but in my mind it is genuine. On one hand, I knew that I was incapable of accepting my parent's death. I also know, for certain, that law and failure to adhere to it were not components of my thought processes ever at that time. On the other hand, I recognize that a law is a law. I was very certain that a law enforcement officer informed me of this too. I find the circumstances of this case so unusual in every aspect. Yet I believe that my sole choice became dealing with it, despite what I knew, despite how I or anyone else felt about it. During all this, I wondered if people would view me as a bad person. I often contemplated also their opinions in thinking that I made a bad decision.

When I consider this, I choose not to view any of this from either of these two perspectives. Rather than this view, I see myself as an individual who was incapable or unable, for various reasons, to do what I was supposed to do especially as society demands. I firmly believe too that I was possibly unstable, unable to react, a bit unstable at that time. I do not like the negative connotations associated with these words, but I know that I could not have been in my right frame of mind. I firmly think also that I was in shock and in denial, and despite all these descriptions, I still have been identified—even judged—as a horrible person by society, by the overall projection of some of the media, and even by individuals who were once very close to me. I have found that individuals have seemed to report stories or issued statements about me in the most negative terms ever. I have also experienced actual members of society who have avoided me, who have judged me ruthlessly, and who have told me that they would never discuss any portion of this incidence with me. I have even found some members of my own family, who know me better than anyone else, have had nothing to do with me since all these events transpired.

As I think about all these reactions too, I only wish and desire that each one of these persons realized that something—something really wrong, devoid of my personal fault—caused my reaction or nonreaction to my mother's unacceptable and unexpected death. I want all of them to know how unfair I found their failure to even consider that fact. As I think further, I just wanted some of these persons, whom I believed concentrated so heavily upon their known and decided aspects of the event, to know that I feel that only a partial part of my story actually occurred. I would even make them aware that I just want to shout aloud over and over again this: "Do any of you realize or care that I just lost the most important person in the world to me—my mother?"

I too would adamantly tell them that this was the other part of the whole story that I believe was neglected by so many that were ignorant of or failed to ascertain or accept the other circumstances of the situation that took place. I have always felt too that no one is to judge a book by its cover. Similarly, then, I think it true that one does not judge a situation or event in the same manner. I take acceptance to that fact with regard to reporters, especially. With their chosen profession, I declare that such a job involves getting both sides of the story in order to have accurate reporting. Likewise, if I think that one side in a reporter's story cannot be contacted, then before introducing his byline to the world, he should hold printing that story until both sides of the facts are at hand. I consider this my personal advice to any media coverers of my situation. I hold to this view so diligently because I feel that failure to do this can affect the life of the one being reported tremendously. In my opinion, it can seriously ruin someone's life. I know this firsthand because, in this whole mess, I experienced that in some ways. I know too that even at the very least, it can damage someone's reputation or create one that is untrue. Lastly, I feel that such negligence can simply make another person's life more difficult than it already is.

My biggest concern is that none of the stories posted my viewpoints regarding the event. The following were not printed until way too late: I loved my mother more than anything, we had a close relationship—an extreme understatement, and I would have never harmed her ever. The reason I know this too is because for any beginning written stories, no one asked me. The first time such an article existed was not until the last article in my local newspaper. I agree that a court decision may be the final word in a case, whether I like that ruling or not. That does not change the truth and other circumstances, however, and the fact that other actualities concerning the case should have been discovered or revealed long before the decision itself. I believe this, unfortunately, happens often in cases—more often than it should, and I feel that it is a bold flaw in our society, especially with regard to criminal cases.

I wished to see my side presented in the first written coverage of the happening. Why did this not occur? I asked the local newspaper reporter myself when he finally contacted me. He stated that no one was home when he dropped by my house. "Oh, my!" was my initial response as he stood outside to speak with me. Then I became furious, and I could feel the redness on my face and a sense of warmth there also. I thought that he should have waited for me or have printed that initial story in a different light. I practically shouted to me that his quotes were not all factual. For example, he indicated that I was placed behind bars on the day that I went for questioning. I stated this to him, and he claimed that the detective said this. I lost my cool enough to shout that this did not happen. I added, "I know because I was there!" I remember telling him that it was only fair to get my side of the story too. I also declared that I was not the bad person whom he portrayed me to be. At some point, he asked for a formal interview. Later, I declined on the basis of caution. He asked if my lawyer had urged me to decline. I answered, "I did not say that." Nevertheless, a story was printed in the next day's edition, claiming that I said that I was not a horrible person. I could only think that my refusal to be interviewed was meaningless. He only contacted me too, because I first reached out to him. I called and left him a phone message regarding his failure to talk to me.

Neither will I get over the fact that the closest local television station in my hometown never contacted me during the entire situation but reported it anyway. I am sure that many people may retort that this is usual procedure. I don't care, and I say, "Put yourself in my place in this particular and unusual situation." In anyone's situation, for that matter, I do not think any one of us ever knows if we truly get the full story from any media story anyway. I am not blaming the media personnel totally for this either. Whoever the media contacts on the matter, I believe, may not be giving the full truth himself. That person's version may often be slanted in favor of only one side too. How do any of us really know? I believe that is why it is so important to contact the other party involved in the matter. That would have been me in this particular scenario, but before the first story ran—and it did run—sadly, I was not contacted prior to that.

I do need to state, however, that I appreciate that last local newspaper article that stated that I agreed to a charge of no harmful intent toward my mother. That, at least, was printed here. Therefore, I know that all of us should live in a country where both sides and more of an issue should be known by society at large. Yet I realize, disappointedly, that truth and fairness often only exist in a utopian society or perfect place. I agree, but that does not mean that these cannot happen. I wish everyone would strive to those ideals. In my incidence too, I somehow missed the wide coverage of that familiar phrase, "Innocent till proven guilty."

In my case, however, one other thing for which I may never have the answer perplexed me. This was when the detective on the case stated, in the last newspaper article, that he believed that I had no "malicious intent" toward my mother. I am grateful for this opinion, yet two or three days prior to my final court date, this same detective contacted, by phone and in person, two members of my family to secure their testimonies against me. I lie not when I tell you how this whole event puzzled me. I am uncertain if law enforcement felt I would plead to a lesser charge or would go on to trial. I mostly think the latter. I reiterate here that pleading guilty to anything bothered me to the utmost, but I did so to relieve myself of the entire situation. I disagreed with any of the charges really, but I had no guarantees with an upcoming trial. I add too that I would have liked nothing better than a trial in which I was found innocent. I like to think that I took the lesser of all the evils surrounding this case.

When it was finally over—the court case itself—I had to bite my lip and move on. Move on to what? To the greater evil, in my opinion, of somehow trying to come to terms with this whole happening. Besides the hurt involved with all this, I still have to face my lonely life without my mother in it. I find this far worse than the former, but both of them have almost literally and spiritually killed me. With regard to the detective's action, I have to admit that it bothered me a great deal. In fact, it disgusted me. I must state also that my family members declined to testify against me. Their reasoning was not because of their familial ties with me either. It was based on the pure and true facts that no such harmful intent ever existed in this case. Had my family members been hauled into court—as they were told that they might be—their statements too would have been that they, unfortunately, discovered the horrific scene of my mother, that they did not know of her death, and that they properly called authorities with an added concern for my own personal safety and well-being. I must state that would have been their complete revelations. There would be nothing added since they know how much I loved my mom and looked out for her. More significantly, they knew that I would never harm her in any way. Even the people in my life who know me are completely aware of this fact.

At this time, I feel a strong need to state again that denial, failure to act, shock, fear, and other aspects prevented me from letting my mom go. I add too that I am certainly sorry for all this. I also claim that God knows this also because I have already discussed it with him. When I think about it now, I never even had to reveal this final thought to any of you because that conversation was between me and my Savior. I will say, however, that I once again could not handle my mother's death in the manner that most individuals would have and especially in the manner society expected me to do so. I defend that too on the basis that no one ever knows how they will react to a certain event until it actually takes place. I then, in my mind, ask everyone if I deserved to be judged as horrible, as a murderer, as one who took no action because, as someone actually said, my mother failed to have life insurance?

I also question society at large by wondering if I also deserved to have my picture and story plastered all over the local newspaper, the Internet, and in fact, all over the world. I would add to this last interrogation these important words, "Just because of my unusual reaction to this tragedy" and without being spoken to as the initial story went out? I believe each of you already know my opinion. It also seems that none of this matters since despite my total desire to avoid any of it, all of it happened anyway. In summary, I know better than anyone that it all happened and may still possibly be news elsewhere. My fear also is that it will never be forgotten by others, despite many other facts at hand. I already know that I will never forget any of it. What I beg from others, however, is to review everything before hastily judging me or anyone else for that matter. I emphasize that even God forgives! I repeat too that I have never even received a traffic ticket, nor have I been arrested in my life for any crime, felony, or misdemeanor, at least not until now.

In this whole media frenzy, I honestly believe that most of the basic facts did not surface, and if they did, I too think that sensational headlines and nonfactual statements overshadowed them. And yes, this immensely mattered to me. I can truly say it still does. I know, likewise, that all this makes me angry. In fact, it makes me much more than that. I am embarrassed by what took place, but I am mostly sad and dejected by the overwhelming coverage of such a tragedy—but what in many ways should have been a private affair, but wasn't in my life. An attorney, viewing the situation, told me that, "It's nobody's damn business what you did when your loving mother died." I couldn't agree more with this statement, and it actually sums up my feelings regarding the entire situation. At the same time, I realize, or at least later, that I broke a law—a law that I never knew existed, much less failed to adhere to on purpose. I reiterate that law and its repercussions never even crossed my mind. I only thought that after my mother's death, it had not really happened at all.

Upon further and later review, the failure on my part to obey the law was more than a shock to me. I honestly had no clue what I had actually done. Yet I feel that I was punished in more ways than one for what I did not comprehend that I did. I also know that after my realization of the so-called facts at hand, I tried to do the right thing because that is how I truly am. My mother brought me up that way, and believe me, I hated to disappoint by doing the wrong thing. As stated earlier in this book, I attempted to contact legal authorities to answer whatever concerns and questions they had, but I never received any return phone calls or visits from any of them on the actual day/night that my mother's body was discovered. I had no contact with law authorities at all until my vividly described arrest in a previous section of this book. The significance of this brings two thoughts to my mind also. First of all, I had never been in legal trouble of any kind, and it never occurred to me to go straight to the police station for interrogation. I, instead, called for an appointment, but my requests were ignored. I would be lying if I said that a phone call back was not necessary. I believe it was. How was I supposed to know when the proper persons with whom I was to speak were available?

Another thing that bothers me too is on my mind. I will try to explain it now. On the third day after Mom's discovery, I received an unexpected phone call from someone—at four thirty in the morning. He phoned to let me know that my story and my photograph were on the front page of the local newspaper. I was completely astonished! I remember, at that time, frantically calling three other individuals—a friend, a pastor, and my counselor. Although I know it was privately shocking to hear of my situation, they outwardly reached out to me with support. I ridiculously never even considered that my story would air publicly. I just never considered this. I had had a traumatic experience having to be ushered to the police station, but a small amount of relief that this much was over had settled me momentarily. I felt that I had candidly spoken with officials and first learned that I had broken a law of which I was totally unaware. I admit that this morning's press coverage pushed me over the edge in many ways. I do not believe that the blast of media coverage ever entered my mind because I was completely ignorant of what happens in such a criminal case.

I mean I do know this happens, but when I was the person involved for the first time, I never entertained any such considerations. I honestly felt that my life had, once again, fallen apart. I could not see a clear way to put it back together again. During all the aforementioned phone conversations, I was frantic, beside myself, and uncontrollably emotional. After hanging up, I remained the same. I was also somewhat suicidal and even admitted this in my phone calls. Much later on, I found out that my counselor was so concerned for my personal safety that she called local officials herself to seek assistance with the matter. There was no reaction. No one came to find me or save me, however. I survived because of God's watch over me and familial support. I believe that the system failed me then. Yet I still faced the charge for which I was arrested. I had to act accordingly then in my mind. I firmly believe that the outcome for my life could have been the opposite of surviving. I was so close to never dealing with any of this.

I feel that my invasion of privacy occurred when the news media became involved in my situation. I did not see the morning coverage on television or any other stories. I did, however, observe a television crew parked at the local bank near my house. This crew was vigorously taking photographs of my home—the so-called "scene of the criminal" event, the story of which was captured in the newspaper. I also watched individuals, not even affiliated with the media, drive by my house, slow down, and stare at my residence. This was a horrible experience for me also. I had just come to the realization that my mother was gone from this earth. I sensed that no one cared about this fact in the least. They seemed, to me, too eager to view the home in which I unknowingly, at that time, broke the law for the first time in my life. I think about how sad this whole situation made me feel.

I remember too that my hostility returned again later that evening as I viewed, on television, the news at six o'clock. I was disgusted with the camera views of my house upon which the news crew concentrated. For example, I watched on the screen the perfect picture of the "Private Property: No Trespassing" sign posted on the column, situated at the bottom of my driveway. I believe their concentration upon this was as if they were stating that it was posted to keep others from finding out that my mother's body was once situated there in this house. I actually hung that sign when I received that property over eighteen years ago. I need to state also that the one sign, which the crew so closely taped, was a new one that I purchased recently since the old one was worn. I conclude with these revelations that things are not always as they seem. This is a lesson that has been reaffirmed to me often during this event. Despite all this too I did give this news crew an interview, much to the chagrin of my attorney whom I had not actually met before any of this.

While encountering her later—in a phone conversation after her appointment—I tried desperately to explain that having never been in trouble, I made a wrong decision. I further claimed that I was listening to my heart and not my head. "I only wanted to tell my side of the story," I said, because the newspaper had printed so many nonfactual statements and portrayed me in a negative light. "The newspaper too," I added, "never talked to me before the first coverage or got my side of the story." I felt this was a human reaction to what I considered an unfair and somewhat untrue portrayal of events. I just wanted people to know the truth—that I really loved my mom and intended no harm to her with my unusual and bizarre reaction. I realize now that I never should have given that interview for several reasons. Initially, I was not calm or even in complete realization of the whole matter then. I should also not have spoken to anyone concerning the case but my attorney herself. I further felt that I was a true novice to trouble and handled the situation the wrong way.

I do not really know if my speaking to reporters hurt or helped me. I believe too that human reaction factored into that parade of vehicles also that drove by to just view the so-called locale of the desperate deed—my house—described on television and in the newspaper. I also realize that I have been guilty of this type of reaction, perhaps at different points in my life. When driving and coming upon the scene of a horrible accident or a police incidence, I know curiosity has gotten the best of me. My head always turns toward the event in front of me and not away from them. I believe we are drawn to the terrible, the so-called negative happenings of life simply because of human nature itself. I am not proud of this reaction either, but I now know one thing for certain. When I served as a victim of being viewed as the events took place, it was not so easy with which to deal as curiously staring for answers is. In fact, I found it horrible, hard to accept, and a really, purely unacceptable thing to do. Each time this occurred during my situation—and there were numerous ones of them—it pained me.

I was embarrassed, and I even hid or looked down if I actually was on the premises of where I live when it happened. I even dreaded taking my trash cans down my driveway for pickup day because these curious people stared at me if they happen to pass by when I was doing so. Going into stores, which I once entered frequently, did not always occur because the untruths of the media made me shameful.

The rumors of murder and mayhem even circulated through some local shops I often visited before, and I have not been strong enough, probably humble enough, to buy items there anymore. The negative cloud that media individuals, unaware of the whole truth of the incidence, and other factors, portrayed have caused me to change the methods and the places I go now. Change has never been easy for me either. All this complicates my life now but exists it does.

I have to admit too that a second article in the local newspaper scared and baffled me. Its headline was "More charges pending in case of body concealment." Upon reading it, I was shocked, confused, and scared out of my mind because I could not comprehend what additional charges could be lodged against me. My first reaction, and most likely the wrong one, was to phone the detective on the case and to leave a message as to what possible new charge existed for me. I state that it was the wrong thing to do for the following reasons. I did not just phone one time either. I did so several times. I never received any return phone calls. My human nature told me that the good-natured and reassuring treatment on the day I was arrested no longer existed. What I mean is that I believed that the pleasurable manner in which I was treated during the interrogation phase was short-lived.

I, never getting a return call, fully felt I was now the accused, and the accuser was not answering. I envisioned that the whole situation had now become two-sided with my side pit against his side. It reminded me of all the phone calls that one of my cousins shared with this official. The law enforcement officer told him to get funeral arrangements made quickly and even that he would notify my relative when the body was returned by the coroner—or released by her. I had actually phoned the official regarding this matter, also with no response either. I just wanted to know if there was any news about this. At that time I, never having dealt with such a legal matter, ended up calling the medical examiner myself. She fully answered my questions as I was the next of kin to my mother. I wish I had known to do this initially.

As frustrated and unaware of policy as I was, I now believe it was improper for the detective on the case to speak with me. I was ignorant of anything because of never having been in trouble myself. What I would have sincerely appreciated was a common courtesy call from anyone to inform me of this. Sadly, one never came. My question, by the way, regarding the aforementioned newspaper article concerned the "possible charges pending." This question was finally addressed by my newly appointed attorney. She informed me that if an autopsy, conducted on my mother's body, did not reveal natural causes—as it actually did later—I could possibly face murder charges!

My first thought, seriously, was *You've got to be kidding!* I reacted this way too because of two reasons: firstly, I knew I had not touched—much less harmed—my mom in any manner. Secondly, I was extremely upset that such an article would really appear. As I read it, it kept resounding in my mind that the word *pending* meant *could* or *may face* additional charges. I considered that speculation not fact, but I was pretty certain that anyone reading the article would remember or think one thing—I possibly murdered my precious mother! I do not think anyone deserves to have that probable judgment lodged against him/her, especially when the facts of the case were not received yet. Oddly enough, the case had not come up in court either. I also admit that I learned more about the media, their sources, and reporters' attempts to capture readers with that sensational story—fact related or not—than I ever wanted to know.

That is almost all I will say about that subject because it is most difficult for me to conceive that we live in a world such as this and even more that I suffered as an actual victim of both of them myself. I honestly could never have even dreamed that this whole event would happen in my life. Bold and negative news sells! That is what draws society closer to the situation at hand. We are curious and hell-bent on finding out more about the most terrible stories to which we are subject. The large number of popular crime shows on television and in papers, on the Internet, and in movies pulls us into viewing unlike anything else. More of them keep surfacing also, and any news is chock-full of these types of stories. They scare us, they sicken us, but we are totally attracted by them nonstop. In the news ones too the facts may not all be there or incorrect, but these steal our attention anyway. These interest us and consume us more than they should.

Some of the responses to my story were mean, ugly, and down-right hateful. That makes me dejected, sad, and sorely disappointed. I must state, however, that there were many positive comments also. I am more than thankful for these. Another positive note also was the newspaper headline that quoted me as stating that I am not a bad person, even If I did not realize that I was being interviewed at that time. Unfortunately, I believe it came a little late. The personal damage, I think, had already been done!

In my opinion, the best newspaper article to me that seemed to present me in somewhat of a positive light did not occur until after the court case ended. At this time, I read about how I pleaded to a charge that did not include or involve "malicious intent" against my mother. In it, I read that even the case detective stated that he did not feel that I had such intent. I was informed by a friend also that one of the local news stations issued statements on Facebook that claimed that authorities said I "apparently could not handle the death of my mother." As much as I finally appreciate these sentences, this is what I kept saying over and over again at the initial start of the case. I believe that we are so eager to catch someone doing something wrong that we do not concentrate on seeing someone doing the right thing.

Although in this situation I did not do the correct thing, I feel that extenuating circumstances did prevent me from doing the right thing. I, once again, could not let her go. What makes me sorry and sad the most is that no one ever printed this until the court case ceased. It would have possibly come out if I had been asked before that first local newspaper article was released. A very wise and supportive friend of mine perhaps sums up this chapter's concern for getting the word out. She told me, "Today's news is quickly for-gotten—replaced by the next news cycle. Everyone who knows you knows the kind of person you are. The people who don't know you don't matter. They are all wrapped up in their own difficulties and don't have the time to dwell on anyone else's troubles for longer than it takes to watch a segment on television or read an article in the paper. It is purely prurient interest anyway."

I say *amen* to her words, and I cannot thank my friend enough for taking the time to tell me her precious thoughts. She added, "I hope someday that someone will appreciate how much and how well you took care of your mother." After having a good part of my life made known to the world, I have had to wonder what my future would hold. Questioning how my life will be after all this publicity has monopolized my time quite a bit. I have also been concerned with my plans in continuing to live my life. I hope the media will not play a role in a negative light in any of my future! I quite frankly have had enough publicity to last a lifetime.

# CHAPTER NINE

# Blessings of Undying Support

I will make them and the places around my hill a
blessing. And I will cause showers to come down in
their season; they will be showers of blessings.
—Ezekiel 34:26

I have read in *Webster's Basic English Dictionary* that when one receives a "blessing," it makes that person happy— "invokes happiness upon them." Like many of you, I know that hymn, "Showers of Blessings," and I know that all of us would love to have blankets of blessings upon us. I believe that, most of the time, we do. I am unsure, though, how often we recognize them with thankfulness. I realize also that these blessings can come into existence in times of greatness and in times of sadness in our lives. I hope that I am overwhelmed with gratefulness regarding these, no matter what is taking place in my life at that moment. I feel this would please God immensely.

Having experienced this bizarre, uncertain, and tragic situation that I have tried to capture in this book, I can honestly declare that there are more magnanimous blessings headed my way! They were so powerful, much needed, and even unexpected, but they came. I must admit too that it was a bit unbelievable for me to conceive initially, but I assure you that they arrived almost every single day, and sometimes there were multiples of them at one time. Pardon the pun, this fact was a "blessing" in itself to me. Hence, the title of this chapter, "Blessings of Undying Support." I chose this heading because one day, during my time experiencing the situation with my mother, I felt so dejected and sad, so I took out several blank sheets of paper. My intent and final action to catalog all the blessings that I had received during this event. Honestly, I did. I had always heard that doing this helped one to feel better, and for me, it worked. It helped me to realize that some good persons still exist in this hate-filled and selfish world of ours. It also gave me the burst of hope needed to continue to survive in life. Now I want to describe them.

At a Sunday church sermon, it was so ordered by God too for my pastor to speak upon the subject "Friends." I believe that this recitation, along with all the above-mentioned blessings to be discussed, was orchestrated by God. I mean that he allowed them to be part of my life, right at the time that I needed them the most. I spoke with my pastor about all the blessings that had encircled me at this time. We talked about the creation blessings which God gave to all of us in a short span of time—seven days. When my pastor told me that the significance of the number seven is completion,' this expanded our conversation of blessings. He said that God created our world in a span of just seven days. I knew this already, and I considered it a true miracle. When I thought about his introducing completion into our talk, I thought that my ability to edge toward handling this situation would not be complete without these blessings—the gifts of undying support from the Lord himself.

In many ways, I believe that the numerous blessings came at the appropriate time, but without them, my healing would never be complete. I know that I probably felt the lowest emotionally at this time in my life than I have ever felt. If individuals had not gravitated toward me to help in some special way—whether it be moral support, actual items, or simply listening. I would have felt all alone and would not have wanted to bounce back from any of the things I was enduring. Without them, I probably would have given up, shut down, and not survived very well at all. God knew this as he knows all—and he was not done with me yet. That is the best way I can justify my desire to make it through this now. He cared enough for me to do this. I could never repay those blessings that he ushered my way. Yet I know that he is the reason all this happened to me. A miracle? You bet.

I include in this chapter the following Bible verse from 1 Thessalonians 5:11: "Therefore encourage one another and build each other up." This sums up exactly what type of blessings I have received and continue to receive presently. The encouragement and the "building up" have occurred in many different facets, however, and they have been, as said before, countless in number. In order to share these, I have categorized them into categories.

Initially, I wish to detail the gift of friends or friendship that I have received. In my pastor's sermon, he gave a description of a true friend. He explained that a genuine friend is not in the friendship for "self." In other words, this person is not self-serving in the least. Some good adjectives to describe a true companion include faithful, loyal, and honest. These traits too are so positive in nature, and I believe that they are some of the traits that God ordains for each of us to possess. My pastor further explained that a true friend can be trusted with everything and values God. This person also wants the best for other friends, values a friend's total interests, defends that interest to the utmost extent. Additionally, this individual loves, respects, and supports others. In connection with support, he or she fights for and with another friend and is even willing to risk everything for that associate. In this friendship too one friend never turns away from another, and that friend does not take advantage of his/her companion either. Rather, the genuine friend can act as an intercessor, who prays with others and demonstrates a "genuine care" or concern for those who so desperately need it. How does that translate in a general sense? The true friend in this world does what is good and right, especially as this friend values God immensely. What a tremendous cluster of traits this person has, and how fortunate to have one in your life, such as this one, who shares missions and values with you, which ultimately create a mutual relationship of like minds that agree with each other! In summation, this true friend bonds together with you, and when this occurs, success is extremely possible. In my personal case, this true friendship, bestowed upon me at the most tragic time in my life, pushes me toward the survival that I so need and desire right now. It enables me, whether step by step or leap by leap, to experience some joy again, despite unfortunate circumstances.

The true friends in my life at this time have given me tremendous advice and incessant support. They have listened to me, and they have talked to me. They have, likewise, checked on me and made me feel better when I needed that. These genuine beings too have given me my space when I so desired, while intervening at the appropriate moment to pray, to uplift, and even to share like circumstances with me. They have blessed me more than I even feel I deserve. They have also texted messages of love and support to me, often turning my loneliness into a feeling that an entire cover of compassion and comprehension actually exist for me. What a feeling this is! They have even wished me peace and sincerely hoped that it would come sooner rather than later in my life. I appreciate that desire for me more than anything because I sincerely want it also. I believe it is my key to experiencing the joy that God and others cherish for me.

Gifts have also been "blessings of undying support" for me at this phase in my life. These too have been numerous and have varied in origin. They include monetary gifts, cards, presents, books, home-cooked meals, special time with others, smiles, positive comments, and the gift of gab. More of these too include Bible verses, hugs, perfect advice, a place to stay, and special sermons that more than touched my heart, Bible studies that do the exact same thing, and many prayers, and even groceries to eat, along with miscellaneous presents that are useful and enjoyable all at once. It is very obvious that the outpouring of blessings has been huge and varied. Each of these has also allowed me to adapt to all the negativity associated with my precious mother's death simply because they have been so optimistic in nature. They have helped me grow spiritually, have given me the gift of necessities, have demonstrated to me what kindness and compassion are. They have literally blown me away. Why? Because they, no matter what they were, have pushed toward having hope, toward living again, and toward believing that God is in control, no matter what, and despite any circumstances. He will see you through—despite everything. I know that the gifts, given to me at this time, will also result in gifts to the senders. After all, Proverbs 11:25 states, "Whoever gives to others will get richer; those who help others will themselves be helped."

Another blessing during this time has, no doubt, been my ability to perform various tasks that were necessary to continue my life. This support, unusually enough, has in some ways come from me. It might even be called blessing myself with ways to assist me through my tragic situation. I am proud of myself when I realize that at several points during this time, I was close to ending my own life after my mother's life abruptly ceased. The fact that, through the help of God and his plans for me—including groups of others to support—I was able to rise up and stand up for me in this manner is quite remarkable to me. What tasks were able to convince me to perform? I sorted through items in my house and simplified my life by trashing what I did not use and keeping what I did. I, through no other power but divine intervention, was able to author my own mother's memorial service and solicit others to help me carry it out. Difficult and sad as it was, it helped me in some ways to heal and to have a degree of closure. I was even able to carry out various obligations, like obtaining birth certificates and altering proper paperwork, like bank statements, to fit the situation. These jobs were not easy to accomplish, and they often evoked the aforementioned stages of grief in me. Yet it was necessary to complete them, despite the anger, unhappiness, and sometimes denial feelings that appeared.

Lastly and briefly, some of my family members have chosen to desert me during these terrible and horrific events, for some reasons that are known but also unknown to me. Even family can hurt you when you least expect it, unfortunately. Yet some of my other relatives have blessed me with their support in more ways than one. I am truly grateful for these "blessings," even if I feel abandoned by some others. God is always good, though. In fact, he is the best friend we can ever have. I am thankful for this gift. Without it, I could not even begin to survive!

# CHAPTER TEN

# A Testimony of Survival

Don't be impatient. Wait for the Lord, and he will
come and save you! Be brave, stouthearted, and
courageous. Yes, wait and he will help you.

—Psalm 27: 14

Sometimes I wonder how I survived and continued to survive this entire situation. I think, perhaps, with a total cluster of events and an entire group of people who stuck by me through the thick and thin of it all. I know too that God is the one who orchestrated all these individuals in my life to assist. I have no doubt about that. My proof of this also is dual in nature. Initially, my Christian background and upbringing assure me of this fact. Secondly, God's promises in the Holy Bible dictate the evidence. In the book of Psalms, chapter 34, I read, "I sought the Lord, and he answered me, and delivered me from all my fears." I also know that in verse 6, it further states, "This poor man cried, and the Lord heard him out of all his troubles." I prayed during this entire situation, and my prayers were certainly answered. Remarkably too, others prayed for and with me. My prayers, of course, were not responded to all at once. I realize that they were answered in God's timing, not my own, but almost daily, at different intervals, and amazingly enough, as I needed them to be. I do not take credit for any of that because I have a strong belief in what the Bible states in Psalm 121: 1–2. Here are the words I read, "I will lift up my eyes to the mountains, from where shall my help come? My help comes from the Lord, who made heaven and earth." The reason for my belief too is that I have experienced such miracles in my life, so many times, that it is impossible to count them. The fact that I grew up in a Christian home is just an added plus to the matter.

I admit that, as human as I am, I have not always believed that the worst of times in my life could transform into better, or even the best of situations. My faith is not as strong as it should be. My ability to surrender all my circumstances, good or bad, to God's control, likewise, is weak. Yet I have done it, and the results have been more than incredible. This situation with my mother's unexpected death is no exception, but it has required more belief and more endurance than I ever suspected to muster. Slowly, step by step, and event by event, I have paved my way through all the unique and tragic times that have come into being. It has never been easy, but I have succeeded—even with baby steps—one at a time. Of utmost significance, I could not have made it this far without the pure intervention of God himself. I shudder to think where I would be without this help—the essential quality I needed to survive.

Survival of this exceptional situation can also be described in many facets. It has, in many ways, involved my whole readjustment to life itself. I compare it to the attempt, if the reader will allow it, to lose weight that some individuals undertake. This task calls for, among some things, a change in one's diet or choice of foods eaten. This may not, all by itself, result in a person's drop in weight. Other aspects, such as exercise or mindset, may also be components to assure weight loss. Therefore, going on a diet really involves a change in lifestyle or way of life. Similarly, in order to survive or overcome—even accept—the loss of my mother in life, I have had to attempt to alter my whole way of living itself. My close-knit family life used to include two persons—my mother and me—and now, on this earth, has been reduced to a clan of one. I do not find that fact easy to accept. Initially, I have experienced difficulty in adapting to the loneliness that I now constantly feel. This feeling often overshadows me at night because I was used to having my mother in the house with me. It is often too quiet, and I have to create noise in the atmosphere with the television set or stereo system—sometimes all night long.

I grieve constantly concerning the loss of my mother too. I have experienced those stages of sadness, anger, and denial, but I have not mastered the acceptance level yet. I do not believe anyone can clearly state how long that will endure for anyone who has experienced such a loss. I often find myself pass through the various grief phases and then revert back to them at other intervals. I believe that many triggers for this repetition of grief include daily aspects of life, such as holidays, songs, certain television shows, special events, etc. All these remind me of times I shared with my mother, and it is hard to accept that we will never experience these on earth together again. In fact, these are often so overwhelming that they create days of deep, deep depression, uncertainty, and an inability to function with regular, daily tasks easily. Overcoming these negative effects is often achieved by me with various activities. For example, I may be unable to celebrate a holiday we spent together, and I do not decorate for it or attend services that are part of its celebration. On the other hand, sometimes I reiterate in my mind the good memories we shared at this time or glance at photos, if available, to remind me of the past happy times.

Aside from loneliness and grief, this loss leaves me sometimes feeling that I do not really have a purpose in life anymore. Previously, the majority of my time was spent caring for my elderly mother as well as caring for other members of my family. My days are often not busy as they were, and I find more freedom than I really desire. I do enjoy being free, but I detest extreme idleness all the time. I will admit, however, that sometimes I do not feel like doing anything either, but I consider that a part of the aforementioned stages of grief. When these times become overbearing, I go outside on my porch just to sit and breathe in the fresh air. I write or read or spend time with friends. I even listen to music to calm my being. I go shopping when able, watch a favorite movie or television show, and even rest when I feel the need to do so. I believe these activities are all keys to my survival of this loss, no matter how minute or significant they may seem.

Corny as it may sound, since the loss of my mom, I thank God every day more and more for the pets in my life. I could not spend a single minute in my home right now without the presence of each of them. As much as they depend upon me for necessities, like food and water, I depend upon them immensely. They comfort me and make me feel a degree of security by just being there. They love me unconditionally. They make me laugh sometimes too. In essence, they take care of me just as much as I take care of them. I truly believe that God created them for these purposes. In fact, they have made my survival of Mom's death possible.

What is my overall goal in reference to this tragic situation? It is, of course, my testimony that I am surviving—edging toward overcoming, little by little, each day. I may have lost my mother on this earth, but I will never ever forget her because she will always be in my heart. I wish to live the remainder of my life with God directing my path of life, whether it includes good or bad happenings—and believe me, it will consist of both. Ultimately, I do not want to waste my time but put it to good use doing whatever God delegates me to do. I would consider those things my purposes now. I want to see my mother and other loved ones again in the afterlife. Initially, I wish to strive for living as much as possible on what I refer to as an even keel, as opposed to that roller coaster of emotions and failure to overcome bad happenings. In other words, I want to survive in the best sense possible by experiencing that real *joy* that God not only desires for me but promises to me in the Bible. The following two verses come to my mind and express this idea. First of all, Jeremiah 31:13 reads, "For I will turn their mourning to joy and will comfort them and give them joy for their sorrow." Secondly, in the New Testament, it is stated: "But thanks be to God, who always leads us in triumph in Christ, and manifests through us the sweet aroma of the knowledge of him in every place" (2 Corinthians 3:14). Verses fifteen through seventeen continue with "For we are a fragrance of Christ to God among those who are perishing; to the one an aroma from death to death, to the other an aroma from life to life. And who is adequate for these things? For we are not like many, peddling the word of God, but as from sincerity, but as from God, we speak in Christian in the sight of God." What a testimony all of this and that will be! I will proudly share his word with those whom I encounter. My experiences too can assist others in surviving and let them know that hope in the middle of all these horrific events will come again.

In this book, I want the reader to understand that my answer to survival of this entire happening is one word—God. I could not honestly have made it without him. In my mind, I know that it has not been easy to get to any point of surviving this without the help of God. In other words, he is my answer to everything, and this situation has been the worst to handle. Yet I do know that he is the reason I have taken steps to overcome the tragedy. I often forget that he has always been there for me. This is a true fault that I have—a weakness in forgetting that he is the key to overcoming anything. He has loved me, he has supported me, he has sent those to me with help, and he has forgiven me. What more could I ask for?

God has enabled me to, little by little as said before, come to terms with what has happened in my life. He has also initiated a path for me to follow in order to start healing. I have come to believe that serving God, praying, reading scriptures, and obeying him are the keys to this success. I have also determined that I was going to try to the best of my ability—as difficult as it would be—to get past this situation. Lastly, I decided that I would attempt to come to terms, as much as possible, with the terrible loss of my mother. I sincerely felt that this task, no doubt, would be the hardest project to undertake. When Mom and I listened to music together—and that was quite often—I always played songs by the country band, Lone Star. In many ways, I would like my plans to include trying to do what this song of theirs says. The words are "When you love someone, you've got to let them go. I'm going to smile because I want to make her happy. Laugh so she won't see me cry... Laugh, so she won't see me hurting... I'm going to let her go in style, and even if it kills me, I'm going to smile." I truly hope that I possibly can do what that song says. I know it is how I want to survive for her. I also believe that she would want that very much. She will, however, always remain with me. I cannot forget my life with her and the joy that we experienced together.

CHAPTER ELEVEN

# A Lasting Tribute and Personal Reflection

Moms hold their children's hands for a
little while…their hearts forever.

—From a plaque

This is a tribute, long overdue, to my beautiful mother. When I say beautiful, I mean beautiful both on the outside and the inside. She was so young-looking that many mistook her for my sister. How happy that made her! It only made me feel old, but secretly I shared this same opinion, and I was so proud of her! I was proud simply because she was my mother. I loved the fact that she had an outward beauty that was expressed with a flirtatious look as she batted her beautiful God-given brown eyes and shared excitedly some opinion on any subject matter or some story from the past. This physical beauty was evident in photographs taken from childhood to the exceptional elderly woman she became. She wouldn't even be caught without her juicy red lipstick! The world found her beautiful too, and she was popular among classmates and friends. She was an exceptionally hard worker. I like to think of her as a true people person for most of her life on earth—enjoying conversations of laughter, jokes, and sharing family stories throughout the years.

She was excellent at remembering dates—including births, special events, and so many times shared with others. Rosey, as she was nicknamed by family and friends, worked hard all her life until her health prevented her from doing so. Like all of us, she also experienced hard times and endured them with much courage and strength. Of utmost importance, however, Rosey had a heart of gold, and when she was able she took care of so many people during her lifetime. She still, however, delighted in listening to her favorite music—mostly country in nature—and watching television, especially Alabama Crimson Tide college football games. Her most enjoyable activity was teaching her daughter, her niece, her nephew, her great niece, great nephews, great-great nephew, and anyone who would listen, these words, "Roll Tide Roll."

She often wore her Bama T-shirt and jacket and sweatpants during those sporting events. Once, as a resident in a nursing home, she dressed as an Alabama cheerleader for Halloween. It was one of the most memorable experiences of both of our lives. My comfort now is how much happiness doing this brought her in just one single day. I can never forget this experience either, since she turned what could have been a negative event in a nursing facility to solid joy in life. That is so precious. Just seeing the smile upon her face will be a forever gift that I will always think about too. This team dedication was such a significant part of both our lives. I am thrilled that she could demonstrate it to those with whom she came in contact on this holiday. The true happiness it brought her alone was enough for me.

I categorize my mother's last years on this earth with the following: "Die-Hard Alabama Crimson Tide Fan," "Country Music Lover,"—especially with Conway Twitty's "Hello Darlin'," "Compassionate Giver to Her Family," and "Appreciator of Good Food and Good Eating." The single most important title that she held for me—besides Mother—was "True Believer in God." She prayed every day and watched devotions on television when her health prevented her from going to church. She often told everyone whom she encountered that God would take care of everything because he always does. She would repeat, "Pray, pray, pray." Her favorite Bible verses included Philippians 4:13, which reads, "I can do all things through Christ who strengthens me." She also adored 1 Corinthians 13:4–13. It states, among other things, that "Love is patient, love is kind. It does not envy… Love bears all things, believes all things, hopes all things, endures all things…" Some of her favorite hymns included "In the Garden," "He Touched Me," and "Because He Lives."

From a personal standpoint, Rosemary was Joni's "Mom," her best friend, and her "world." Needless to say, they were extremely close and spent endless hours together. Rosemary took care of Joni Walker, the two names she desired her to be called, and Joni Walker took care of Rosemary. "Rosey" even encouraged Joni to treat house-hold pets like family, because she said that was really what they were. To these animals, Rosemary herself was known as "Granny Ma." With this name, Rosemary became a grandmother to furry friends rather than to children. She loved playing this role too.

To say that Joni and Rosey loved each other would be an under-statement. In fact, they always signed cards—given to one another on special occasions: "With love always and forever." From birth to adulthood, Rosemary brought her daughter up as a single par-ent. She spoiled her rotten but also instilled in her a work ethic of responsibility. Rosemary consistently taught her daughter numerous things. She even asked her daughter to remember that "All men are created equal" and to always treat people the way she would want to be treated. She assisted Joni in learning numerous Bible verses, how to spell new words, and about the importance of reading books at an early age. She once told Joni that a church congregation was shocked to hear Joni recite "The Lord's Prayer" at preschool age. Rosey beamed with pride too, at teaching Joni Walker to spell *chrysanthemum* when she was little. Rosemary bought numerous items for Joni, and among them was a little blue book, which, page by page, introduced the Biblical verse Joshua 1:9 with complete illus-trations. This verse reads: "Be strong and of good courage; be not afraid, neither be thou dismayed: for the Lord thy God is with thee whithersoever thou goest."

This verse has given Joni much comfort in times of fear and will forever be impressed upon her mind. It proves too that Rosey intro-duced Joni to Jesus at an early stage in life. Along with many happy adventures in the world, Joni's mother taught her that life has its disappointments also. For example, she shared with Joni the following poem, "Little Blue Boy," by Eugene Field. It reads:

> The little toy dog is covered with dust,
> But sturdy and staunch he stands;
> And the little toy soldier is red with rust,
> And his musket molds in his hands.
> Time was when the little toy dog was new,
> And the soldier was passing fair;
> And that was the time when our Little Boy Blue
> Kissed them and put them there.
>
> "Now don't you go till I come," he said,
> "And don't you make any noise!"
> So, toddling off to his trundle-bed,
> He dreamt of the pretty toys;
> And, as he was dreaming, an angel's song
> Awakened our Little Boy Blue.
> Oh! the years are many, the years are long,
> But the little toy friends are true!
>
> Ay, faithful to Little Boy Blue they stand,
> Each in the same old place
> Awaiting the touch of a little hand,
> The smile of a little face;
> And they wonder, as waiting the long years through
> In the dust of that little chair
> What has become of our Little Boy Blue,
> Since he kissed them and put them there.

Joni even chose this recitation for an English project in high school. Her teacher remarked to her mother what maturity this compositional choice demonstrated on Joni's part. The educator had made this comment before regarding books that Joni read and summarized for class, such as *The Other Side of the Mountain*, by Evans

G. Valens. This book is about a skier, paralyzed in an accident, and facing life after such a tragedy.

None of the frustrations that I endure, however, could compare to the sudden loss of my mother on this earth. What would I say to her if she were still here? A great deal. From a negative standpoint, I would selfishly cry out, "Why are you not here?" and "How could you leave me?" Then, I would emphatically state that, "I wish you were here with me right now, in our living room, beside me doing whatever we used to do." I would tell her that, "If I only had one more day with you, I would appreciate you more." I would tell her too how unexpected it was for me to realize that, on that early morning, it would be her last day on earth. I would further emphasize how unfair this world can be because I miss her more than anything, and I, only thinking of myself, want her back here with me. I would want her to desperately know that it is too hard to try to live without her. I would say that I have never been as lonely in my life as I am without my precious Mom. I would even let her know that all our pets miss her too, especially Haley, our dog, and that none of us really understand why she is gone.

I also would tell her that I do not know how I will face any holiday without her since those were extremely special times we shared together. I would declare to her how I cannot begin to comprehend how to go on with my life without her. I would say to her how scared I am to face whatever time I have left because she was the one on earth closest to me. I would remind her that she was always there for me, no matter what. I would talk about how much I miss her good advice and the methods by which she handled everything—through prayer to God—and told me to do the same, even if I felt it was hopeless.

I also would explain that, most of all, I miss those famous words, which she demanded from everyone: "Roll Tide Roll." I would let her know how I cannot imagine ever watching a Crimson Tide football game without her by my side. I would want her to know that I miss the meals we had together, the shows we watched on television, and the talks we shared regarding every subject under the sun. I would I would make it known that on the morning I lost her, my heart broke in more than a million pieces, and like Humpty Dumpty, I don't think it can ever be put back together again. I need her to know that when she died, I died too. I would make her realize that I would love, even just one more time, to lay my head upon her chest and let her hold me as she did when I was a child, sometimes an adult, when I was sick, and when everything went wrong. I would share with her that I miss her presence every single minute of every single day. I would also say that I miss her most when I am in our house alone and at night.

During the evenings too, I would tell her that I can't really sleep, and I have to have the noise of the television or stereo just to remain in the house. I would want her to know that I detest the fact that she is not here for me to talk to, and that when I find out something, such as my cousin's awards or the death of someone, whom she knew, I cannot let her know immediately, like I used to be able to do. "I still want to share everything with you, Mom," I would declare. I would also make her aware of my seeing some ad on television or my hearing some song, reminding me of the great moments we had together.

From a positive standpoint, I would tell her that although I miss her immensely, I know that it was God's plan for her to leave. I would declare that I comprehend more than ever what she used to tell me all the time: "You only have one mother." I would add that I am so glad that she does not have to suffer or feel pain on this earth anymore. I would want her to know that I am so happy that she does not have to fear anything either, including storms, where everyone in the family is, and if they are okay, and that while walking she might fall. I would exclaim that I envy her not having to be worried about those mundane and major happenings in life, like paying bills, what are we going to eat or do today, or what next problem will arise.

I would let her know how wonderful it is for her to meet God, our Father, and to reside with him. I would hope also that she will get to see the loved ones we share who will go there too. I would say that it must delight her to see all our pets who are no longer on earth, especially Spooky, who lived the longest of all of them and touched her heart the most. I would even share with her that I will always remember the things that she taught me and to be extra grateful for each of them. I would tell her how thankful I am that God gave me to her and her to me. I would not have wanted it any other way. I would share how I respected her honesty, dedication, and hard work toward any task she endeavored. I would say how proud I am that she chose to raise me as a single mother and put her whole heart and soul into it. I would state that I respect and thank God for everything she ever did for me—in good times and in bad times.

I would let her know that I could never have the special relationship I had with her ever again, and I miss that tremendously. I would also make her aware of how many others miss her also, and of how many individuals have reached out to support and help me in various ways at this time. I would state that they all say I'm going to be okay, but I still do not believe that. I would want her to know that I went back to church, but it is often hard to remain there because she is not here with me anymore, and it is hard to share things with her. I would play all her favorite songs for her and diligently listen as she sang with them, no matter what it sounded like. I also would want to watch her dance again since she loved it so much. I would tell her that it gives me some joy to look at photos of the past and to think about all the trips to the Smokey Mountains and to Florida, which we took years ago. I would say that these pictures make me sad some of the time also. I would even remind her that I still have those two pictures of her, with me as a little girl, and when she wore her bikini and looked like a professional model.

I would also share my gratitude for having found the little book that she wrote to my eldest second cousin. I would let her know how I have read it over and over again and delighted in all of the memories she retained of everything in all our lives. I would let her know that, because of her inspiration and because of a friend's suggestion, I wrote a similar book for my little third cousin. She would adore that fact.

I am fifty-seven years old now, and I find facing Mom's death the most tragic and unacceptable thing that I am supposed to do. Everyone tells me that my mother would want me to be happy, but I can only think of the joyful times we had together. I find myself believing that I really do not have a purpose in life now. You see, my major one was taking care of her and others around me. I miss cooking for her after she taught me to cook. I miss hearing her say these words, "Be careful, call me, and hurry back," as I went out the front door. I even miss those zillion phone calls she made to me, while I was gone, just to check and assure herself that I was okay. Oh, if I could only have one of those phone calls right now. It would literally mean the world to me. Her asking if I made sure all the doors in the house were locked would, likewise, be something else. I also miss combing her beautiful black-and-gray hair and handing her all her makeup necessities, red lipstick included, to use for the day. I wish she could be present for me to say one more time how beautiful she really is. I also miss that wonderful smile that she gave me after I made these remarks.

How do I find joy out of this, what I consider the worst event with which I am supposed to deal? Truthfully, I do not know. I do realize, however, that it is a roller-coaster ride every single day with some moments of happiness always sprinkled with instances of sadness. I am having the most difficult time letting her go. I even find myself shedding numerous tears as I write or read these words in this chapter of my book. I really want this entire happening to be a nightmare from which I finally awake. When I realize this too, I want to see my cherished mother sitting in her recliner, as she always did, living life on this earth, side by side with me. The fantasy in my mind wants this, but reality tells me that it is not going to happen. I am slowly trying to figure out the ways that I can somehow really accept that she will no longer coexist with me in this world. Yet it is really difficult to do so—so much more difficult than I ever expected it to be. When individuals tell me that I took good care of her, I always think of something that I did not do more of but should have. Similarly, when they say that God will reveal my purpose in life now to me, I feel skeptical—not because I do not believe in God, but because I am so unsure of myself.

With my mom I felt security, a closeness that can never exist again, and a deep love and gratitude simply because she was my mom. It is very overwhelming to lose all those qualities at once. In life, I have experienced over and over again that the goodness of life can come out of the badness. Yet this whole time, I never knew that I would be facing what I have always dreaded to face and what I have always wanted to believe would never happen. I thought truly that my mother would be sick right before she actually died and maybe in a hospital. It is not that I desired that; it is just what I thought. I did not ever consider that her death would be in a split second on a morning a few days after we celebrated Christmas together. We had spent time with other family members on Christmas Eve and had a wonderful celebration then, and the holiday after.

To accept this, many people have told me that it will take one step at a time or day by day to recover. I agree, but it is so frustrating to progress slowly step by step, and then, suddenly, to reverse that progression and revert back to an overwhelming state of grief once again. It is doubly hard also to return to that place of darkness, experiencing the familiar feelings of sadness, depression, and hopelessness regarding the situation. My pastor has told me to keep my focus on the Lord and not to allow other thoughts to distract me or depress me. He also assures me that God will help me and give me strength. I know he is right, but I'm not completely there yet, and I do not know how long it will take me to do so—even if I completely can. He also says that it is harder for some people than others to surrender all their problems to God. This is a result of human nature. I believe it to be true too, because I am one of those who struggle with that. Another good friend tells me to stop worrying about things that may or may not happen. That's good advice also but hard to accept when most of my life I have been a worrywart, recalling all the adventures or events that I have endured. I have found a real peace in accepting that good things can exist after bad happenings. That's why I truly believe the Romans 8:28 promise in the Bible.

It reads: "And we know that God causes all things to work together for good to those who love God." Yet this current situation has me totally baffled, and with it I do not have that precious serenity that I so desire. I hope I will, but I do not know if that will ever happen. Apparently, it takes longer for some people to fully trust God than others. As I stated, I have been able to do it with various situations, but it never seems to become permanent for me. What I mean is that I do not achieve that peace and joy that God desires for us. When another crisis arrives, I let both of these things slip away. I don't want to, but I do. I know that this is not fully accepting God's control over my whole life, but happens it does.

I pray for the day that with this hardest struggle that I have ever tried to endure, that calmness and joy, will return one day. Then they will be there forever in my heart. I also pray that I can give control of all things in my life to him who made me. The reason why? Because I cannot do it myself. He is stronger and more powerful than I am, and he will freely deliver me if only I choose for him to do it. I thank God too for the best mother anyone could ever have. I want her to truly rest in peace. I know that she is with God now, but I will get to see her again one day. The entire life that he has enabled me to share with her was the biggest blessing of which I know.

My relationship with my loving Mom was a gift that I received on day one of our time together. She largely made me who I am today, and my significant thanksgivings regarding this are indescribable. Yet they exist. She taught me many things—including the presence of God in my life. She loved me. She cared for me. She brought me up to thank God for everything in my life, good or bad as it may be. Now I face the rest of my life on earth without her. I still do not comprehend all the ways to do this. Because of her, however, I have also found love in the form of the strength that he has and gives me to endure the biggest tragedy in my life.

It is present in the answers to my prayers that he gives me, but I remember these answers are in his time, and they may not be what I expect or want them to be. Yet they are the best ones for me since his love for all of us is that compassionate, that strong, and that ever-present. His love for all of us exists also in the people whom he puts in my path to help me, especially when I am going through the worst of times. I know too that they can do many things for you, and each thing is unique or different, but it comforts me in a way that brings me sheer joy, hope, support, and even a reason to go on. I believe too that many of these things can be as follows: a smile, a hug, a listening ear, a phone call, a card, a gift, a home-cooked meal, a recitation, a pat, a kind word, a bottle of aspirin, an offer to help with something, a song, a church sign, a bumper sticker, a movie, a book, a sermon, a place to stay… In essence, I believe these are blessings of undying support. This list too could go on forever—which is how long he loves you and places others or things near you to demonstrate His undying love.

"Oh how I love Jesus, oh how I love Jesus, oh how I love Jesus because he first loved me." I feel that those words to that hymn are so true. My mother agreed with this also. I too believe that love is a powerful emotion—so powerful that it can make you do many things. Sometimes, for love, we do silly things like dress up as a mother duck for a school play, simply because we love teaching and our students. Love can also lead you to do negative things, such as taking on more things than you can handle, only to realize that it is too much for you. That strong feeling of love can even force you to do the so-called bizarre or abnormal, like the subject matter that this book describes.

I believe that the most significant love, however, is the love that Christ has for us. It is the most powerful and genuine type of love there is. No one else's love can equal that love either. I know you can believe that a person has the best affection for you, but it can never compare to the love that Christ showed us when he came to earth and died for all of us on a cross. His love is also eternal; it never ends. I, or you, may think it is not present, especially when things go wrong or even when our circumstances are the worst ones that we can ever experience. He and his love are there even if I do not believe it. Where is it? Initially, I found it in his gift of a mother to me. The one he chose was, to me, the closest to perfect that he could create.

My mom demonstrated so many blessings and so much love to me. For all the reasons written in this chapter, and many more, I loved my precious mother. That is the real *truth* why I was incapable of letting go.

Since we died with Christ, we know we will also live with him.
—Romans 6:8

# CHAPTER TWELVE

# Final Thoughts

Upon realization of this entire story, which came later, I'm ashamed as well as uncertain, knowing for sure that I could not come to grips with the actual death of my mother. I simply refused to accept the complicated scenario—I could not handle it. The reality even now is more difficult to accept. Healing and even my digestion of the whole ordeal will not take place all at once, of course. It may take a lifetime itself. I cannot do it on my own. How far I have come now—and hopefully will continue to come—is left by me to a higher power. My path is uncertain, but God will clarify it for me, and believe me, I ask him to do this every day, every hour, and sometimes every minute. That's how much I miss her now. That is also how difficult it is for me to conceive that she is really gone from this earth forever. I had to turn to God more than ever now. He was the only one I knew who would truly help me to survive what I could not accept but have to.

# CONCLUSION

I can do all things through Christ who strengthens me.
—Philippians 4:13

I wrote this book, *Incapable of Letting Go*, for numerous reasons. First of all, the title itself refers to an actual event in my life, the unexpected death of my dear mother, and the circumstances surrounding it. The "not letting go" part demonstrates how I was not able to face this death. It is a true story, as well as the events surrounding it. This was a very difficult story to tell, but I did for several reasons. Initially, I want individuals to realize that people face death in many different ways. There may be society's expected method of doing so, but that does not always take place. Many factors, like undying love, devotion, and sincere closeness, can be a part of that acceptance or unacceptance. I do not believe either that any of us know how we will react to it—or even depending upon whose death it is—until we actually face it. When death does come, as this recitation fully demonstrates, the unusual or bizarre, the uncertainty of events, and even the fearfulness surrounding it can be present. Society can react in different ways to this circumstance of life ending also. So can the legal system, the media, and those people close to those experiencing it. It is also true that, sometimes, what people may think of a situation is not always true. I believe there are always extenuating incidences, as this book details, that only those really close to the situation actually know.

Following such an event too, the issues of privacy, support, and survival are also of extreme significance. Details of these matters are described here also. Lastly, I hope these writings, with all their unbelievable but true details, explain my testimony of survival through the tragic times of life, especially the tragedy—the death—of my cherished and unforgettable mother.

> When I am afraid, I put my trust in you.
> —Psalm 56:3

Rosemary and Jo on Halloween—Rosey dressed as Mary Poppins at
a local nursing home facility—2nd prize for Best Costume there

College football flag sitting in the yard at the Outland
house, purchased at Phyl's sporting goods store

Jo's painted Bama sign, created as a gift by Kathy Bennett, friend

Jo & Rosemary at Daytona Beach, Florida

Jo as a little girl picture, taken by Olan Mills
photography at the request of Rosemary

Jo, Rosemary, and "Rosebud," (blow up fish) at
grandparents' home in the good ole days

Rosemary, seated outside a local motel in Gatlinburg, Tennessee

Rosemary, dressed and ready for high school dance

Jo, Rosemary, and doll, "Chrissy," at grandparents' home

Jo & Rosemary celebrating the Fourth of July

# ABOUT THE AUTHOR

Jo Whitney Outland resides in Bristol, Virginia. She has taught and worked with children most of her life and is currently retired. One of her significant goals is to find the joy in the worst of events that have happened to her, as reflected in Romans 8:28. She claims to have much experience in this area. Her main priorities are serving God, serving others, and writing as much as she can.

CPSIA information can be obtained
at www.ICGtesting.com
Printed in the USA
LVHW111013100221
678919LV00008B/447

9 781662 414305